Washington Geographic Series

WASHINGTON'S COAST

BY ROBERT U. STEELQUIST

copyright © 1987
AMERICAN GEOGRAPHIC PUBLISHING
Helena, Montana

Text copyright © 1987
Robert U. Steelquist

WILLIAM A. CORDINGLEY, CHAIRMAN
RICK GRAETZ, PUBLISHER
MARK THOMPSON, DIRECTOR OF PUBLICATIONS
BARBARA FIFER, ASSISTANT BOOK EDITOR

This series provides in-depth information about Washington's geographical, natural history, historical and cultural subjects. Design by Len Visual Design. Printed in Hong Kong by DNP America, Inc., San Francisco.

To
Dr. John Steelquist
Surgeon, Scholar and Explorer

Clockwise from above:
Black-tailed deer. KEITH D. LAZELLE
Black oystercatcher. JEFF FOOTT
Driftwood, Olympic National Park. PAT O'HARA
Petroglyph whale, Wedding Rocks. KARNA ORSEN

American Geographic Publishing
Box 5630
Helena, Montana 59601
(406) 443-2842
ISBN 0-938314-28-9

ACKNOWLEDGMENTS

I would like to thank Jenny for her constant encouragement; Mark Thompson for his patience and humor; Karna Orsen, whose keen eye, high standards and sisterly affection were all-important in shaping the selection of historical photographs; Pat O'Hara, Keith Lazelle, photographers and companions; Sheila Sandiford, who assembled place-name material; Pat Burkhardt and Terry LaDuron, former colleagues at the Arthur D. Feiro Marine Laboratory; Jim Walton, friend and teacher.

Gracious assistance was provided in Pacific County by Noreen Robinson, Ilwaco Heritage Museum; Kathy Sayce; Bonnie Sayce, Ocean Park Timberlands Public Library; Edie Shire, Washington State Cooperative Extension Service; Virginia Graves, Pacific County Historical Society; Dale Espy Little and Sidney La Rue of Oysterville; and Bill and Jean Nitzel of The Picture Attic, Long Beach. Historic photos from Grays Harbor were made available through the courtesy of Jones Photography, Aberdeen.

Others who generously offered their expertise include: Tom Terich, Western Washington University; Steve Speich, Malheur Field Station; Barry Troutman and Eric Cummins, Washington Department of Game; Hank Warren and Kevin McCartney of Olympic National Park; Eleanor Stopps of Admiralty Audubon; Lucille Munz, who graciously made available transparencies of Zella Schultz paintings from the John. W. Thompson Collection; Iris H. W. Engstrand, University of San Diego; Polly Dyer, Olympic Park Associates; Jan Henderson, U.S. Forest Service; and Buzz Shaw, Seattle Aquarium.

South Beach Wilderness, Olympic National Park. PAT O'HARA

Washington Coast

Contents

Introduction	6
CHAPTER ONE The Restless Ocean	12
CHAPTER TWO The Gentle Land	24
CHAPTER THREE Life of the Coast	38
CHAPTER FOUR Strait of Juan de Fuca	54
CHAPTER FIVE The North Coast	66
CHAPTER SIX The South Coast	78

Right: Shipwreck near Shi Shi Beach. PAT & TOM LEESON

Front cover photos, clockwise from left:
North Head lighthouse near Long Beach. BOB & IRA SPRING
Harbor seal. JEFF FOOTT
Harvesting cranberries. BRUCE HANDS
In Olympic National Park. PAT O'HARA
Seagulls at sunset. KEITH D. LAZALLE

"...as we proceeded to the north, the coast began to increase regularly in height, and the inland country, behind the low land bordering on the sea shore, acquired a considerable degree of elevation. The shores we passed this morning, differed in some respects from those we had hitherto seen. They were composed of low cliffs rising perpendicularly from a beach of sand or small stones; [and] had many detached rocks of various romantic forms..."

Capt. George Vancouver
April 28, 1792
Between Point Grenville and
Destruction Island
Washington Coast

INTRODUCTION

Right: Brooding in its moods, powerful in its energy, the dynamic ocean shapes Washington's coastal shore and cultural identities of its inhabitants. TIM THOMPSON

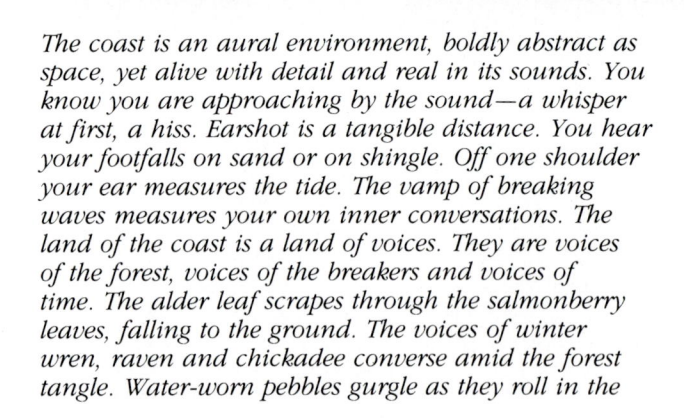

The coast is an aural environment, boldly abstract as space, yet alive with detail and real in its sounds. You know you are approaching by the sound—a whisper at first, a hiss. Earshot is a tangible distance. You hear your footfalls on sand or on shingle. Off one shoulder your ear measures the tide. The vamp of breaking waves measures your own inner conversations. The land of the coast is a land of voices. They are voices of the forest, voices of the breakers and voices of time. The alder leaf scrapes through the salmonberry leaves, falling to the ground. The voices of winter wren, raven and chickadee converse amid the forest tangle. Water-worn pebbles gurgle as they roll in the frothy surf. Sea lions are barking. There are the voices of canoe balers; whale, seal and salmon hunters; gatherers of clams; singers.

The coast's voices also include those of axe and chainsaw; steam donkey and whining diesel; of the bell that tinkles when a fat coho thrashes against the commercial troller's line or the groan of a power gurdy winding in a crab pot. The coast's voice can be the voice of fury, of ships breaking; of men's voices being swallowed. Its voice can be mild, of breeze in the dune grasses. Its voice can whisper, as breakers distantly roll in moonlight.

PAT O'HARA

Washington's outer coast is a line of demarcation in more than a strictly natural sense. It forms the boundary where landscape ends, with all of its irregularity and texture. It marks the edge of a territory we think we dominate, revealing one beyond that we think we do not, though we do. It reminds us that our world has limits, that our achievement of conquest that brought Euro-Americans to the western edge of "the New World" has ended. The coast is the turning-back point. It asks about the nature of our next conquest, that is, now that we are the continent's inhabitants what form will the habitation take? Must some new territory present itself that we may reach further, or will we content ourselves with grasping the finer points of living with a land, over time, so that it can sustain a rich yield and support subsequent generations with the generosity it tendered the first?

Washington's coastal region is defined within this book as the shoreline from Point Wilson (where the Strait of Juan de Fuca ends and Admiralty Inlet begins) to Cape Flattery, to Cape Disappointment (the headland north of the mouth of the Columbia River). Incorporated within that region is the lowland, with its river valleys, the coastline proper, with its islets and inlets and an offshore marine environment rich in lifeforms and pervasive in its influence on the land itself. The book is divided into several preliminary chapters that reveal the natural and human history of the region as a whole, followed by a series of chapters that present the unique characteristics of three distinct coastal regions—the Strait of Juan de Fuca, the Northern Outer Coast and the Southern Outer Coast. Interwoven throughout the narrative is the assumption of a regional identity, of cultures shaped by a natural environment both benevolent and harsh.

Through time, that identity has been timorous, as when spirit beings loomed in the dark forests and ritual forms made peace between humans and their animal and spirit cohabitants. That identity has also been bold, as when early settlers, far removed from such niceties as law, operated their tiny empires as entities unto themselves and when owning an axe, a steam donkey or sawmill was enough reason to mow as much forest as you could see.

The book is also written to alert us to an overlooked landscape whose time is about due for other developments. It is a world not only of gray whales, migrating salmon and

Above: Twilight at Ruby Beach. Between two worlds, the shore reflects the processes of both contructing the land and reducing it to its finest particles. JEFF GNASS

Left: The Three Sisters, remnant seastacks near Sekiu. Photographed in 1910 by Asahel Curtis.
WASHINGTON STATE HISTORICAL SOCIETY

Top: The California gray whale (Eschrichtius robustus), has made a comeback after being hunted to near-extinction in the last century. Twice a year the barnacle–encrusted mammoths migrate along Washington's coast. JEFF FOOTT ***Bottom:** Rich silt accumulates in Washington's coastal estuaries, mud that harbors more life than the richest agricultural soil.* TIM THOMPSON ***Right:** The North Head light, perched atop a basalt outcrop north of the Columbia River mouth, began service in 1898, coaxing southbound ships away from the treacherous sands of the Long Beach Peninsula.* BOB & IRA SPRING ***Facing page:** North Head.* TIM THOMPSON

a multitude of other animals and plants, but also of scenic scapes that refresh and inspire. It is the realm of a bounty of resources for which claims are being made that challenge present notions of resource policy in Washington. Offshore oil and gas and other mineral resources will become the focus of bitter divisions within our society as some advocate a speedy conquest and others none. The continental shelf, now vaguely somewhere beyond the sunset in most of our minds, will become increasingly visible as part and parcel of the coastal ecosystem upon which much depends: livelihoods based on the living resources of the sea, the natural integrity of the habitats of threatened and endangered wildlife, even that elusive but pervasive cultural factor, "the quality of life." An understanding of that unity must grow if the next decades of exploitation are to leave even as much as the last.

But a coastal identity can be measured in less extreme terms, as shades of gray, as warm pastels of twilight and muted earth tones of forest or outcrop.

Such an identity is formed of a daily presence given to ocean sounds, or gentle rain. Yet given a natural backdrop of such potent extremes, of both a land and a sea that so completely dwarf human scale, of forces that give equal opportunity to dread and piety, of elemental differences so vividly displayed, the coast keeps very basic questions in the attention of its inhabitants. The rewards of such attentiveness are manifold. They consist of breaths of rich air, visions of the infinite variety of light mingling with surface, and voices, voices, that cross time and fill the spaces where human experience has left room for the world to enter our crowded lives.

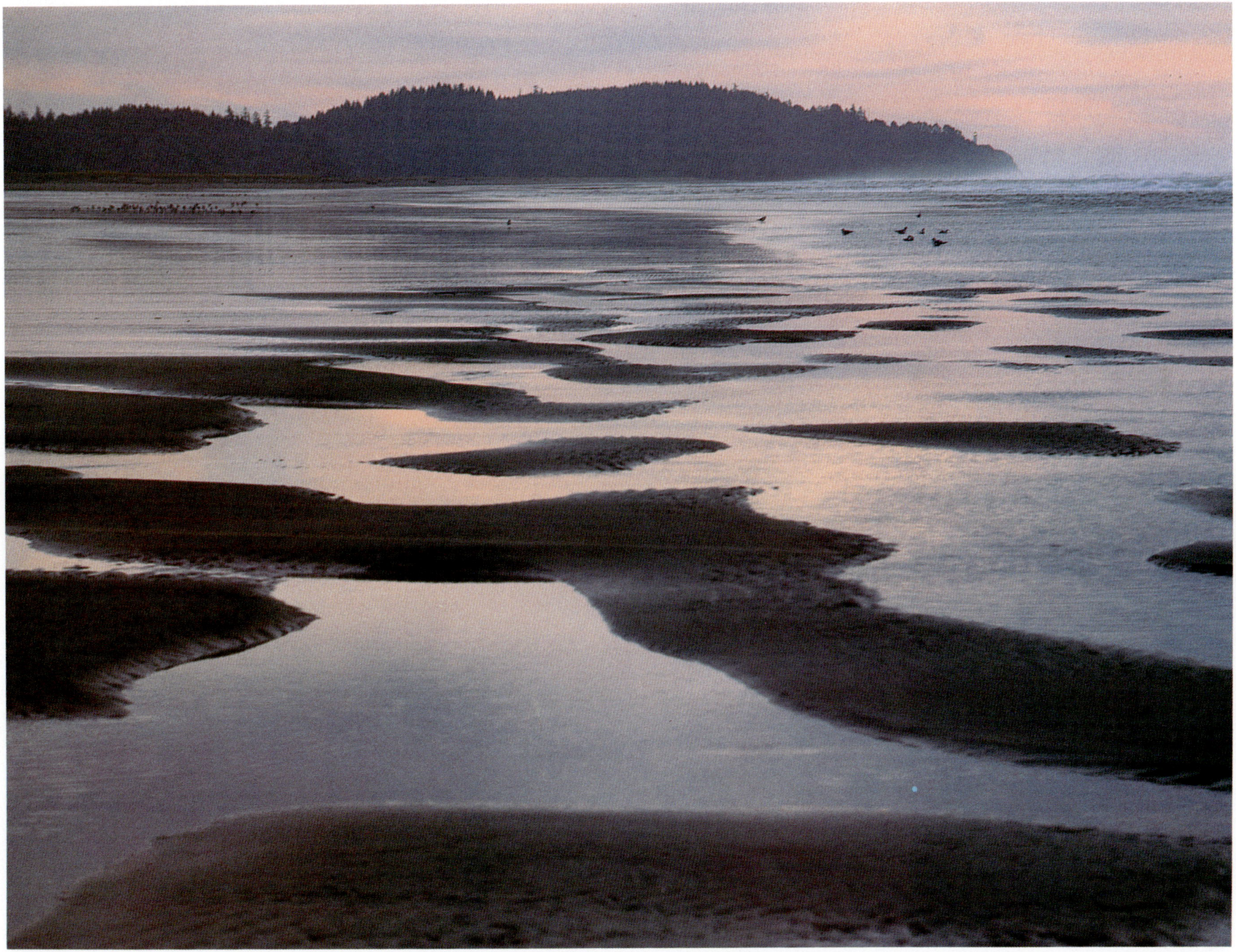

MAKAH WOLF RITUAL

Top and above: Makah ceremonial masks portraying Wild Man. MUSEUM OF THE AMERICAN INDIAN, HEYE FOUNDATION
Right: Physical strength—critical to the challenge of a harsh environment—is still rewarded among the Makah, as here during Makah Days competition. TOM & PAT LEESON

A broad headland rises out of the turbulent surf. Above the pale mists, the summits of Bohokus and Archawat Peaks tower, fringed with ancient gnarled trees. The outlines of the land vanish and reappear in the clouds. The boundary between the firm and the evanescent shifts constantly. The cape is a land of these softened boundaries, where distinctions between land and water, wind and wave, the wild and the tame blur into a unity.

For uncounted generations, the Makah people have occupied the cape, as much at home on the water as on the land. Theirs was a rich subsistence that relied on an innate perceptiveness of the world's workings as much as on human strength and ingenuity. During winter months, the wild drew close around their villages. Darkness edged into the spaces between the houses, bringing with it its consort of terrors. The wolves came in close. And with them, Raccoon and the Wild Man, beings half human, half wild. To guard against the procession of spirit things, and to strengthen themselves for daily trials of survival, Makah people observed a strict ritual—the four days of Qua-ech', the initiation Klukwalle—the Wolf Ritual. In its function, the ritual shaped the collective psyche and forged the tribe's truce with the cape's other beings. It fostered self-discipline and courage in its initiates and it opened the door for participation in other secret society ceremonials.

According to an account of ethnologist Alice Henson Ernst, published in 1952, the Makah Klukwalle shared many characteristics with similar ceremonies of the Nootka and Kwakiutl people north of the Makahs, and the Quileutes, their southerly neighbors—indeed, kinship bonds along the coast were common. In most of its forms, the ceremony dramatized the capture of uninitiated people by symbolic wolves, the captives' receipt of special powers or instructions from their spirit captors, their rescue by tribal members previously initiated in the Klukwalle society, and the collective purging of the Wolf spirit and the restoration of human form to all participants.

Preparation for the initiation began when an important tribal leader decided to sponsor the ceremony and sent "inviters" to families with secret society membership, announcing the day of the beginning of the ritual and requesting their presence.

On the first day, as the sky darkened, the initiates were gathered in silence. With faces blackened and with hemlock boughs garlanded around parts of their bodies, they were paraded from house to house, beginning in the west and ending at the house where the ceremony would be held. The procession was accompanied by the sound of whistles imitating wolves.

On the second day everyone was invited. Accompanied by a bird rattle, villagers sang Klukwalle songs that had passed through the generations. That evening, society members wearing family masks made a procession through the village, led by one or more men with a special wolf mask. As the crowd gathered at the Klukwalle house more rattle songs were sung. Abruptly, the singing stopped. The silence broke with the sound of a lone wolf howling. All present repeated the howl, carrying on the chorus in such a lifelike manner that forest wolves sometimes joined in. Present also on the second night were one or more masked wolves and the Wild Men, who demonstrated their ferocity by circling the interior of the Klukwalle house.

On the third day of the ritual, non-members were told to stay home and warned against peeping. It was during this phase of the initiation that the novices were gashed on the arms, a symbolic act of courage and one that re-enacted the story of Ha-sass, who bled himself to lose his human scent and deceive the power-holding wolves. Near dusk, the society members paraded through the village, wearing the Wolf and Wild Man masks of the second night, but joined by masked Hornets who stung onlookers, and Raccoons who caused general mischief. Inside the Klukwalle house, rattle songs and drumming on a long, wooden box drum set a mystic tone for the proceedings. Initiates, some in pain, danced the wolf frenzy amid loud whistles and wolf calls. One or two dancers portrayed the Frenzied Wolf, careening threateningly about the house armed with knives. Often Frenzied Wolf was prevented from harming anyone only by men who kept him roped during his dance. Following the display of frenzy, the initiates could practice their dances in preparation for the fourth night—the ritual climax.

The fourth day began with a general invitation. Everyone prepared costumes and dances for the coming evening. As dusk gathered, the entire village participated in a massed display of costumes and masks based on myriad animals, heroic characters and inanimate objects. Nightmare Bringer and Basket Woman, Eagle and Woodpecker and many others joined the Wolves, Hornets, Wild Men and Raccoons. The procession moved from house to house, becoming raucous and gathering into it more characters, more masks and more Beings. Singing and rattle-shaking reached a high pitch as the crowd moved through the village, gathering at the Klukwalle house.

Here, they would enter and by means described variously, would be unmasked—an act of becoming human. Certain characters would elude the unmasking for a while, eventually subdued as their human identity was revealed. Each character was "calmed" from his Being state and restored to his human form. Songs were sung, and the initiates would practice dance steps that they would perform on the fifth or following day—their first as members of the Klukwalle society.

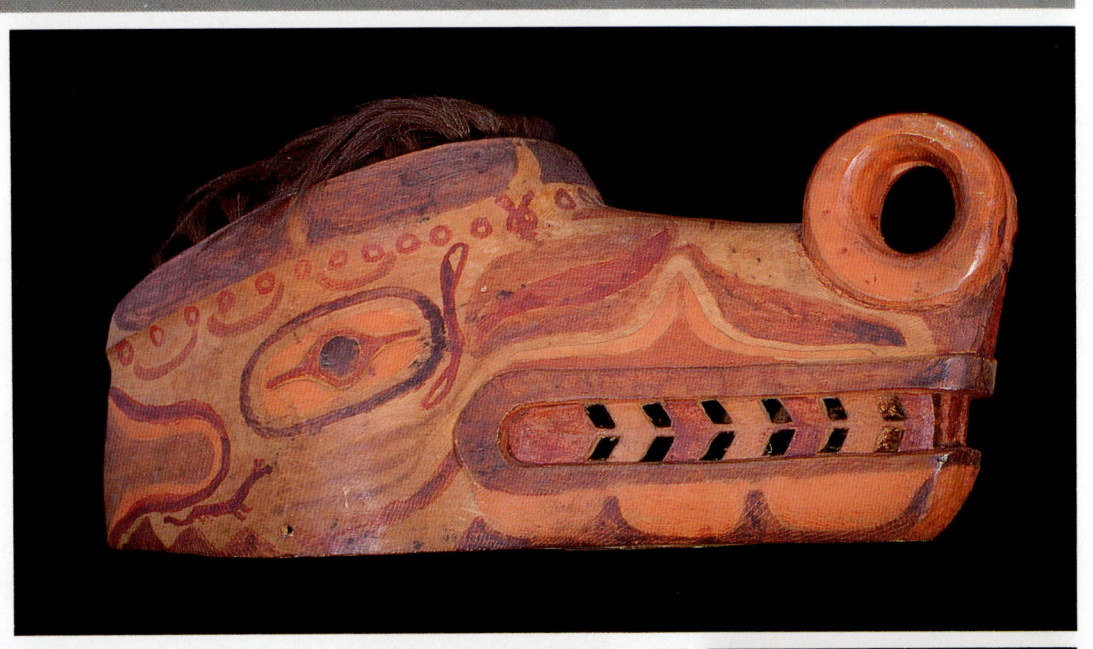

On the fifth day, the Klukwalle members gathered for dances on the beach. This was a time when member-families would take turns dancing their own steps, singing their own songs. Speeches followed—thanks was given and the business of the village life gradually took over. The costumes and masks were put away, the paint was washed from the skin. Newly energized by the ritual confrontation with forces and entities that surrounded them, the Makahs resumed the daily pattern of village activities, of gathering and mending, of preparing for the sea hunt and conducting their human lives.

Qua-ech' represented a cycle of awareness of the Makah, the interdependence of all things, the need in people for the strengths displayed by their fellow inhabitants of the coast land. It was the harmony of voices, the intertwining of the individual psyche with the collective belief of the society; of man with wolf, the natural model of strength, endurance and power, and of mankind with the coastal landscape, with which it struggled constantly to make tenuous peace.

Top: In the Makah Wolf Ritual, humans took the Wolf's form by donning the wolf mask, and reenacted the passing of Wolf's power to the people. Bottom: A Makah cedar headdress used in the Wolf Ritual. KARNA ORSEN PHOTOS

CHAPTER ONE

THE RESTLESS OCEAN

BOB & IRA SPRING

Earth, the water planet. As continents and oceans are born and die, the interplay of sea and land is our planet's dominant cycle. The theme repeats itself in many rhythms—movements of plates, measures of tidal ebb and flow, and the beats of breaking waves. NORTH AND CENTRAL AMERICA FROM APOLLO 16 MOON FLIGHT—U.S. GEOLOGICAL SURVEY PHOTO

Facing page: Relentlessly, waves batter the Washington Coast, eroding prominent headlands and redistributing coastal rocks grain by grain. Washington's rugged North Coast has resisted civilization better than it has the sea. BOB & IRA SPRING

The magnetism of moving water is an attractive force in human imagination. A denser medium than the air we are accustomed to operating in, water moves with weight and purpose, its separate molecules unified in a body that at once attracts and repels. In occupying its space visibly, it symbolizes elements of flux that remain unseen. To some, it metaphorically expresses the way of Everything—the Tao. Certainly each of us, as we stare into charging surf, and hear the rising and falling noise of moving water, is awakened to a deeper sensibility, and connected to a greater whole.

While limited evidence suggests that water plays or has played a role on planets other than our own, we characterize earth as "the water planet." This identity became real as a popular image only when views from distant space revealed just how much of the earth's surface is water-covered. Although abstract percentages had long been available to support the fact, it was the portrait of the rich cobalt blue of the world ocean, the soft white of its polar caps and the lacy mists of its swirling weather systems that gave the numbers meaning. Ours is the planet dominated by water. As a compound, water is the most abundant liquid molecule on earth. As the ocean, it covers more than 70 percent of the planetary surface; as the stuff we are made of, it accounts for 70 percent of our body weight and it constantly bathes each of the 100 million trillion cells of our body. Remarkably, it is salty water—of the same general composition as the sea itself—together with proteins and cells, that forms the blood surging through our veins.

The asymmetry of the water molecule (a lop-sided arrangement of two hydrogen atoms attached to an oxygen atom) gives it a positive charge on one side and a negative charge on the other, thereby creating the attractive force that bonds the molecules to one another. Likewise the ocean itself charges our planet's surface with dynamism in its redistribution of equatorial heat toward the polar regions, its undulating twice-daily response to the pull of the moon, and its complex interaction with an equally dynamic atmosphere that gives rise to climates and weather. And if the dance of substance alone isn't enough, then the part played by the ocean in giving life to our planet and sustaining it in its diversity and abundance declares its role as an organizing force of the highest earthly order. Metaphorically and materially, water in its

A concretion yields its nucleus—a shore crab entombed for millions of years. KARNA ORSEN

Thick-bedded sandstones are worn smooth by the caress of waves. The rounded sculptural objects are concretions—cement-like balls formed as concentrations of cementing material gathered around foreign particles. CINDY McINTYRE

Facing page: Headlands of the Olympic Coast consist of erosion-resistant sedimentary rocks between 15 and 22 million years old. KEITH D. LAZELLE

collective form—the hydrosphere—represents a fundamental source of unity and diversity in the planetary system of the earth.

Origin of the Sea

The age of the earth is speculated to be 4.5 billion years; its oldest rocks, about 3.2 billion years. The oldest ocean floor appears to be a youthful 200 million years. How old is the sea itself?

According to theory, water that now comprises the ocean was produced as a volatile gas, given off by volcanic activity. Thermally released from chemicals bound within rocks that formed slowly in the newly congealed planet, these "excess volatiles" condensed into water as they cooled. Estimates place the continued addition of water to the earth's surface at about 0.1 cubic kilometer per year. None escapes the gravitational pull of the planet. Thus, the amount of water on the surface of the earth is constantly, if minutely, growing. Its distribution among the ocean, polar icecaps, and the atmosphere—the three most important reservoirs on the earth's surface—has varied through time. During Ice Ages, when icecaps and continental glacial systems have expanded, global sea-level has been lowered. With global warming, sea-level has rebounded.

Periods of residence of water molecules in the various reservoirs vary greatly. A water molecule may be in the atmosphere for nine days, fall as rain, course through a river system in two weeks, remain in a large lake for 10 years, percolate through a shallow aquifer for decades or hundreds of years and rest in the deep ocean for 3,000 years. Locked in the Antarctic icecap, it may reside for 10,000 years. Eventually, it completes the cycle and begins another.

The ocean basins themselves are quite young. They also display greater similarity in composition than the older continental masses, which vary widely in their substance. While the older margins of the basins often are littered with sedimentary overburdens of considerable thickness, their spreading centers are only thinly covered with sediments. Recently formed basalt (heavy volcanic rock often associated with underwater eruptions) is evident along the mid-ocean ridges, contorted in extruded forms called "pillows." Like water itself, the crustal material that underlies the ocean basins is constantly being recycled. It oozes out of volcanic vents along the mid-ocean ridge and forms new sea-floor. Over millions of years, that sea-floor moves toward a collision with another plate.

When the collision occurs, the sea-floor, being heavier, is drawn under the edge of the other plate and is re-melted as it is forced down.

Our current ocean basins have formed roughly in the span of time since the breakup of the last great supercontinent, Pangaea, which began about 200 million years ago. Slowly divided by spreading action centered along great rifts, Pangaea was broken into five major continental blocks. According to the distribution of terrestrial fossils, "fossil" magnetism, correlation of rock types in widely separated regions and other means, geologists have tracked the present continents backward in time and reconstructed the creation of the ocean basins that now separate them.

According to such reconstruction, the youngest ocean basins include the Red Sea, the Gulf of California and the Atlantic Ocean. The oldest fragment of ocean basin crust appears to be about 175 million years old and is located in the northwest Pacific, very remote from the present spreading center of the East Pacific Rise.

In the vicinity of the Washington coast, the spreading center—the Juan de Fuca Ridge—occurs about 300 miles offshore. Crustal basalts dipping beneath the continental shelf are no more than 10 million years old. The East Pacific Rise along the entire western coast of North America is a series of short ridge sections, broken and offset along large transform faults. Transform faults occur where one plate slips past another side-by-side, either moving in different directions or in the same direction at different rates of speed. The Juan de Fuca Plate, one of the smallest of all the plates now in motion, is bounded to the north and south by massive transform faults and on the west by the Juan de Fuca Ridge and on the east by its subduction trench, where it is being forced beneath the North American Plate. Movement of North America along its present course will one day override the Juan de Fuca Ridge, smothering the diminutive Juan de Fuca Plate. The ridge itself will remain active and that portion of North America that crosses it will be torn away and carried toward the northwest, just as parts of coastal Southern California are being skidded northward along the continental edge today.

As with other relations among parts of a whole, ocean basins and continents are but reflections of each other,

Point of Arches, Olympic National Park. KEITH D. LAZELLE

and the processes that give rise to each are shared. The slow-motion dance of continents drifting over the viscous mantle is also the birthing of seas. Only timeless water itself has endured longer than the crust upon which it rests.

Movement of Water and the Face of the Shore

Just as dynamic forces within the earth's mantle give rise to the interplay of its general crustal features, imbalances in physical and chemical conditions of the seas, along with the earth's spin and attractive forces of other solar system bodies, create instability and change. This instability results in a complex set of ocean-atmosphere relationships that include high and low pressure systems, prevailing wind patterns, ocean currents and waves. So closely linked are these interactions that separation of cause from effect is rarely possible. And, however complex the dance of these physical forces among one another, their influence on biological systems compounds the intricacy many times over. The likelihood of breeding success of a pair of tropical seabirds, for example, may be directly related, through the complicated regulating system of the sea, to weather patterns on continents a hemisphere away.

Major ocean currents represent a significant link between the physical and biological events of the sea. These currents operate as large elongated circles called "gyres," that are driven by wind. Global wind patterns were first observed by early transoceanic explorers, who found that, at sea, wind direction was relatively constant within broad bands of latitude. Within 30° of latitude north of the equator, winds constantly blow from the northeast; within 30° south of the equator, they blow from the southeast. Between latitudes 30° and 60°, they blow from the southwest in the northern hemisphere and northwest in the southern hemisphere. As a result, certain bands of latitude possessed favorable wind patterns for sailing ship movement (tradewinds) and certain boundaries between bands possessed no winds (doldrums). If the earth's surface was completely covered with water, wind patterns would vary only slightly within each latitude zone. Similarly, currents driven by those wind patterns would be very regular, with broad bands of water simply moving in different directions like traffic on a roadway.

This neatly ordered scheme is complicated, however, by the presence of continental masses, which block the even flow of wind and water around the globe. The continents confine the currents to their respective ocean basins, setting up the circular motion of the gyres. In the Pacific, the Japan Current moves west to east at about the middle latitudes, bringing tropical water past Japan and shooting it across toward North America. As this current meets North America, it splits, forming one current that flows south along California and one flowing north, into the Gulf of Alaska. That the Washington coast is affected by the Japan Current is established by the character of some of the floating debris that reaches our shore—glass fishing net floats and, on rare occasion, fishing vessels of Asiatic origin that have drifted across the broad Pacific. Off Washington, there is seasonal variation in the path of the Japan Current, due to fluctuation in latitude of the main body of the current. In winter, when the current lies to the south, the current flows northward; during the summer, when the current crosses the Pacific at a more northerly latitude, it flows along the coast to the south.

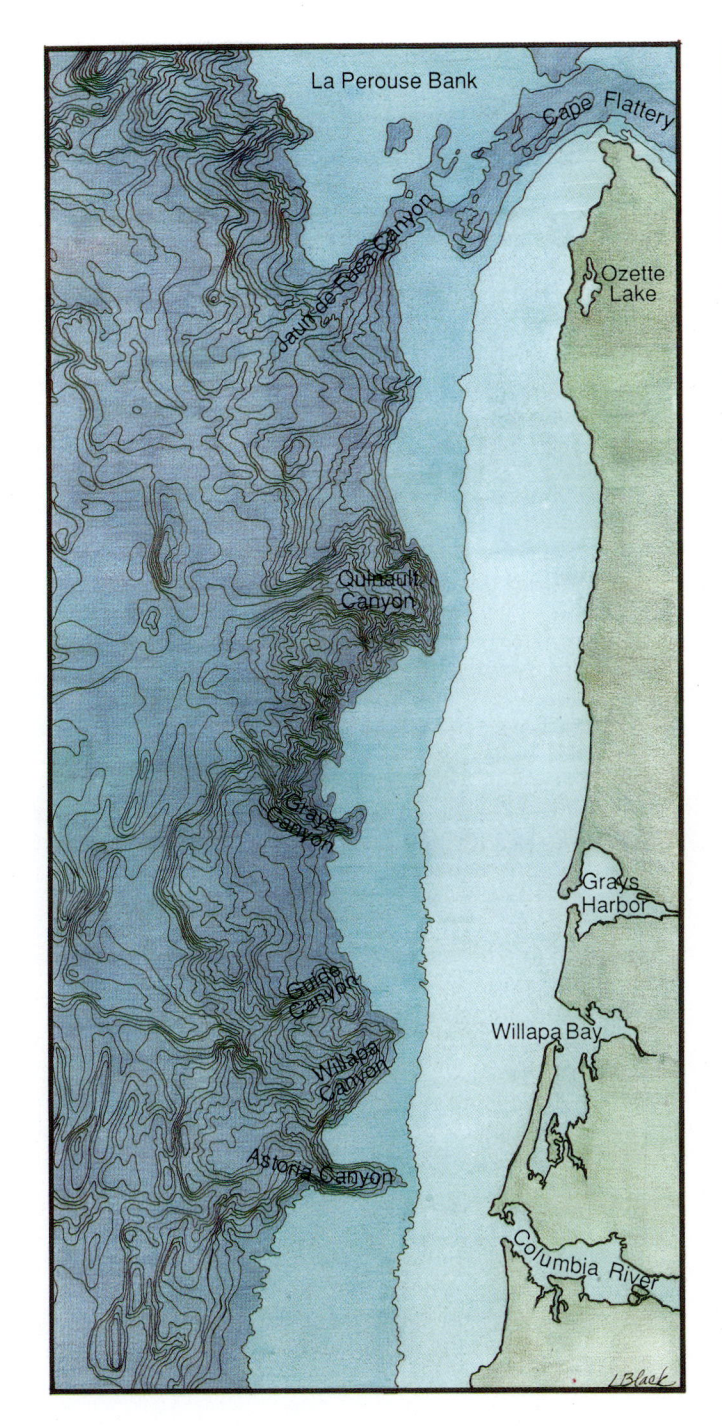

Map: Washington's continental shelf forms an unseen extension of the familiar terrestrial landscape. It consists of a broad terrace approximately 100-200 meters deep near the shore. The shelf "rim" undulates between 50 and 100 miles offshore and is broken by six major canyons. Beyond is the abyss—ocean floor in places more than a mile beneath the surface. Contour interval is 100 meters. BASED ON BATHYMETRIC MAP BY OCEANOGRAPHIC INSTITUTE OF WASHINGTON.
Above: Second Beach, near La Push. The wild North Coast is wildest during winter. STEPHEN TRIMBLE
Left: Oyster-laden schooner, Willapa Bay. PACIFIC COUNTY HISTORICAL SOCIETY

17

North Beach Wilderness, Olympic National Park. PAT O'HARA

Along the coast the interaction of summer winds, which typically blow from the northwest, and summer current flow creates a condition known as "upwelling." Upwelling is the movement of cold, nutrient-rich water from deep regions beyond the continental shelf upward, where it replaces warmer surface water blown away from the shore by surface winds. The mixing of the mineral-rich "deep" water with the warm, sunlit water at the surface nourishes a multitude of marine organisms that includes simple one-celled phytoplankton and the entire food pyramid of organisms that is built upon the plankton foundation. Although upwelling along the Northwest coast is not so strong as in other regions (such as western equatorial South America), it nevertheless remains an important cause of the biological richness of the coast.

Currents and wind patterns not only shape the complex web of life found in our coastal waters, they also shape the face of the coast itself. Where water and land meet, a gradual, unrelenting transformation process is underway. Piece by piece, the shoreline is altered by the various forces at work in the dynamic ocean. Both erosion and deposition are at play, with broken rock pounded fine into particles of sand, laid out into the nearshore current and settling to rest on some bar, beach or spit. In endless combinations of conditions, sea forces dismember, then reassemble, the shore.

Shorelines possess a life, with characteristic phases of youth, middle age and senility. That lifespan is marked by a tendency toward smoothing, in which headland features erode and inlets fill. The youthful coast is one characterized in its geology by ruggedness, where a sea-level rise has drowned a landscape dissected by the erosive power of running water, creating prominent headlands and cusps that follow the pattern of ridges and ravines on the slopes above. The cutting edge of the sea is its breakers, raised during high tide to the foot of the slope, doing their violence with bursts of water and air, and the rock and log projectiles they carry in suspension. The water exploits cracks and fracture-planes and scours clean the debris it loosens. Where turbulence of breaking surf pounds at a rocky shore, a distinctive terrace called an "abrasion platform" is carved. These platforms are usually exposed only during low tide and, in some areas of the coast, can extend for hundreds of yards. Good examples are found at Tongue Point, on the Strait of Juan de Fuca; and in the vicinities of Cape Flattery and Cape Alava. Abrasion platforms are particularly rich with intertidal lifeforms—broad surface areas, mazes of surge channels and numerous tidepools create a complex array of niches for hundreds of species of marine life.

In a process called "wave refraction," surface waves run parallel to the shore, curving where a shore curves outward to form a point. Wave energy tends to focus on the extreme tip of the point and erosion rates are actually accelerated there. Eventually, seas pound at both sides of the point forming tunnels and arches. With the collapse of the arch, a sea-stack is formed, separated from the land by a bench when the tide is low, by boiling surf when the tide is high. A stack is sharpened into a pinnacle, standing alone until it collapses. Thus, headlands attract the forces that undo them. Conversely, energy is spread evenly over an even shore and weakened in a concave shore feature, allowing debris to accumulate.

Characteristic of middle-aged shores are cliffed headlands where spur-ridges have been truncated by headland erosion and depositional features such as bay-mouth bars and sandspits of various shapes. Remnants of the former headland may be present during this phase, as offshore islands, particularly where bedrock is relatively resistant. The enclosure of formerly open embayments by bay-mouth bars alters both the energy and salinity regimes within such bays, creating estuaries where riverborne silt fills the basins and saltwater is diluted by freshwater entering from rivers and streams.

Old age in the life of a shore arrives after thousands of years. Irregularities are worn off the face of the land by the hammering of countless storms; the entire shoreline may have advanced inland by miles. In country with relatively homogenous parent rock, the seacoast straightens into long beaches and cliffed headlands. Where a stream or river enters the ocean, the buildup of alluvial deposits may result in the creation of a delta. In country with complex bedrock geology, the differences of density and erosion-resistance of the various formations will become apparent in the coastal contour—harder rock types will repel the landward movement of the shoreline, softer rock will succumb to it.

Washington's coast has four distinct regions, based on the interaction of physical forces of the ocean and geological composition of the land. In each region, this fundamental relationship, readily visible in the face of the shore, also manifests itself in the distribution of marine plants and animals and the degree of hospitality that the shore affords humans. These provinces can be identified by the shape, form and substance of their principal coastal features.

The eastern portion of the Strait of Juan de Fuca consists largely of relatively steep cobble beaches and steep bluffs of soft, unconsolidated glacial debris. Two significant features are Ediz Hook, a sandspit formed by river sediments once deposited by the now-dammed Elwha River, and Dungeness Spit, reportedly the longest natural sandspit

Upturned sandstone bed near Slip Point forms a window in time—a warmer ocean once lapped against the shore. ROBERT STEELQUIST

Vertipectin fucanus, a large fossil scallop, is the signature of the Clallam formation, dating from Lower Miocene time, about 22 million years ago. KARNA ORSEN

Wave action attacks the shore, cutting even faces on short spur ridges. Such faceting is characteristic of "middle-aged" shores. TIM THOMPSON

The dynamics of erosion and deposition sort beach materials. Local parent material and the intensity of wave and current action determine beach composition. WOLFGANG KAEHLER

in the world. The pale bluffs that line the eastern strait represent the edge of a broad coastal plain composed of sand, gravel, clay and compressed glacial till. This material forms a deep mantle over most of the Puget Sound lowland and was put into place during the Pleistocene epoch, when broad glacial lobes poured south from the Fraser River valley. As the Juan de Fuca lobe stagnated, its sediment load was deposited throughout the lowland. The rise of sea-level subsequent to the last glacial retreat flooded the glacier channel and coastal erosion proceeded in earnest in the soft material. The relative youth of these shores is revealed by the frequent exposure of mastodon tusks and tree stumps in the crumbling bluffs.

West of Striped Peak, the shore of the Strait reveals solid bedrock. Outcrops of basalt, breccia and a variety of sedimentary rocks lend irregularity to the shore. In addition, wave energy increases along the coast as you approach the Pacific. This combination creates a condition known as "pocket beaches," small coves and prominent, broken headlands. The pocket beach region wraps around Cape Flattery and extends south to the Hoh River. This region is characterized by the most dramatic and forbidding of shores. Submerged reefs, bared fangs of rock, and steep, enclosed cobble beaches are often inaccessible by land or sea; before the era of the powered vessel and modern navigational aids they were particularly dreaded by navigators. Rock formations along the coast in this region represent some of the oldest on the Olympic Peninsula. In addition to basalts and breccias associated with undersea volcanism, and sedimentary rocks formed within the last 50 million years, rocks associated with a much older (144 million years) continental structure are found at Point of Arches.

South of the Hoh River, geologists describe a "terrace" region along the coast. Here, evidence of glaciation is again apparent in a series of "piedmont plains," upland benches made up of materials transported into the lowland by alpine glaciers of the Olympics as outwash. The flattened surfaces of Destruction and Alexander Islands correspond directly to piedmont surface features of the mainland. Evidence suggests that landward advancement of the shoreline has progressed as much as three and a half miles in the last 6,000 years. Rock formations in this region consist primarily of sandstones and siltstones—relatively soft sedimentary rocks generally less than 40 million years old. Broad sandy beaches also are more in evidence in this region, composed of material from eroding sea-cliffs and sediments discharged from rivers.

South of Point Grenville, the coast is characterized by long expanses of fine-sand beach and associated depositional features like extensive points, spits and bars. Other very complex and striking coastal features of the sand region are the two large estuaries, Grays Harbor and Willapa Bay (Shoalwater Bay) and the Columbia River, whose influence on the shape of Washington's south coast is profound.

Grays Harbor represents a well-developed estuary in a recently drowned outwash channel that now carries the Chehalis River. The Chehalis River valley owes its width to the many-braided rivers it carried as it formed the drainage outlet of the melting Puget lobe of the Cordillerian lowland glacier. The Willapa Estuary and its sister feature, the Long Beach Peninsula, are quite young. As the Long Beach Peninsula formed over the last 7,000 to 10,000 years, the sea retreated, ceasing to lash directly at the sedimentary toes of the Willapa Hills. Gradually, the estuary has formed, drowned by silt from the eroding hills and filled with shoals by the gentle shifting of fines in the relative calm of the enclosed bay. The vast sediment load of the Columbia River contributes a high volume of the material carried northward by currents that travel along the shore. Even in the historical era, accreted lands along the Long Beach Peninsula have grown— primarily because of the addition of the North and South Jetties to the mouth of the Columbia River.

Each piece of the Washington Coast offers its own evidence of the almost-organic relationship between water and rock, wave and shore, continent and abyss. What we must know as we stare into the surf, lost in thought, is that each wave is but part of the earth's first motion, an echo of a fundamental imbalance that resonates through the earth's flowing mantle, its liquid cover, The Ocean, and its evanescent atmosphere. Each burst of a wave is connected to the explosion that formed the earth and the moon, and the explosion that daily lights our sky. Our planet has not rested since its first day, the jostlings of its crustal plates and the motion of its waters are its work.

Although the shore often represents the interaction of the sea and the land in its more energetic forms, the interplay can also be one of delicacy and subtlety. PAT O'HARA

JUAN DE FUCA RIDGE

Plate tectonics theory forever altered our perception of the relationship between the workings of the ocean-floor crust and the birth of mountains. The Olympic Mountains—ancient seafloor basalts interlayered with sandstones and shales of the ocean floor—rise distantly between La Push and the mouth of the Quillayute River. TIM THOMPSON

Few ideas have altered our awareness of the forces that shape earth more than the plate tectonic theory. Taking scientists and the lay public by surprise in the mid-1960s, plate tectonics combined old ideas with new observations, and gave rise to a radical view of continents inching over the earth's crust, driven by the upwelling of molten rock deep in the planet's mantle.

The theory itself was no less a puzzle than the diverse natural phenomena it sought to explain. As pieces fell into place, a working explanation emerged for the great Rift Valleys of Northeast Africa, similarities between fossils found continents apart and the unexpected youthfulness of ocean-floor rocks. And for all of the theory's global implications, a crucial piece of evidence was gathered off the Washington Coast along the Juan de Fuca Ridge.

Theories of the movement of continents have been advanced for centuries, many associated with images of the biblical deluge, others with the cataclysmic separation of the moon from the earth. In 1915, Alfred Wegener, a German meteorologist and explorer, proposed a theory suggesting, from evidence in similarities between the continental shelf outlines of South America and Africa and in rock strata series on either side of the Atlantic, that the continents of the New and Old Worlds had once been joined. His theory was dubbed the "Continental Drift Theory." To British and American geologists it was heresy. Nevertheless, the theory had its friends, and although it failed to win general support in Wegener's lifetime, it would not quietly retreat into obscurity as its detractors hoped.

World War II ushered in an era of rapid advances in technologies well suited to undersea exploration. Wartime needs for methods of detecting enemy submarines led to the development of instruments capable of plumbing the ocean depths and faithfully recording bottom contours. Later development of the astatic magnetometer, a device to measure the orientation of relatively weak magnetic fields, opened up a new branch of geophysics called paleomagnetism, the study of "fossil" magnetic fields found in volcanic rock. Using the tools of paleomagnetism, scientists were able to determine the age of volcanic rocks by measuring the orientation of the rocks' magnetic fields against known shifts the magnetic field of the earth as a whole. In learning the age of seafloor basalts, early paleomagnetic investigators were startled to learn that ocean floors are characteristically made of materials fewer than 200 million years old, a span that accounts for fewer than five percent of earth history. Contrary to beliefs held by the majority of geologists of Wegener's day, that the ocean basins were among the planet's oldest geological features, scientists of the 1950s discovered that they were among the youngest.

Discoveries amassed at a remarkable pace. Painstaking assembly of bottom contour data collected throughout the world's ocean basins revealed a global pattern of suture-like ridges of extremely young rock—mid-ocean volcanic rifts from which the seafloor appeared to be spreading. Magnetic profiles of these rift areas revealed amazing symmetry. Rocks on one side of the rift appeared to be the same age as rocks the same distance from the ridge on the opposite side. Detailed studies from highly specific localities in different oceans seemed to be pointing to the same conclusion—that the rifts were seafloor factories and the movement of oceanic plates away from these volcanic cracks could be the driving mechanism for Wegener's discredited wandering continents. Yet even the discoverers were cautious, wary of extending their theories further than the evidence would support.

One investigation that lent critical support was a study by Arthur D. Raff and Ronald G. Mason of the paleomagnetism of a 280,000-square-mile region off the coast of Oregon, Washington and Vancouver Island. Here, the East Pacific Rise approximates the contour of the coastline, about 300 miles offshore. Raff and Mason made detailed maps showing the striped pattern of young oceanic basalt, flanked on both sides by seafloor that gets progressively older as distance increases from the rift. Where it disappears beneath the continental shelf off Washington, the ocean crust was a mere 10 million years old. The research revealed that with the exception of large faults crossing the rift at right angles, the pattern of symmetry was carried out faithfully from Cape Mendocino to the Queen Charlotte Islands. Nowhere had such mapping covered as large an area and proven so clearly the fundamental principle of seafloor spreading. Coupled with research being performed by an entire generation of geophysicists, the discovery of the Juan de Fuca Ridge helped establish the theory of plate tectonics and restore Wegener's theory of continental drift. With a powerful new model of the earth's dynamism, the puzzle revealed an elegant solution.

Wegener had been ahead of his time.

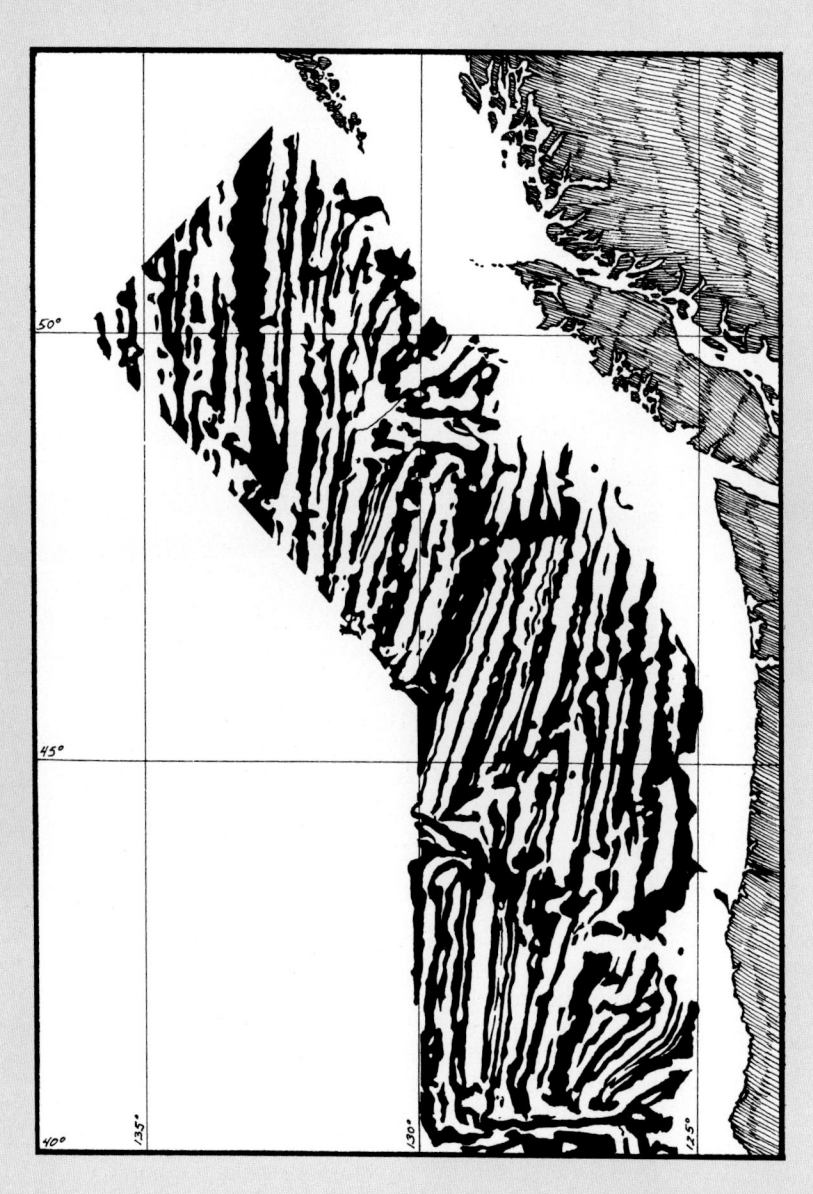

The bold pattern of stripes is a fingerprint of the earth's magnetic field over the last 10 million years, recorded in the basalt seafloor off the Washington Coast. The black streak near the center approximates the location of most recent seafloor spreading activity; alternating black and white stripes show reversals in the earth's magnetic field mirrored on each side of the spreading center. Black is normal magnetic polarity; white is reversed polarity. The black streak nearest the Oregon coast represents rocks formed about 10 million years ago. Basalts closer to the land are buried beneath thick sediments of the continental shelf—their magnetic properties undetectable.
(AFTER RAFF AND MASON)

CHAPTER TWO

THE GENTLE LAND

The spotted owl (Strix occidentalis).
© GARY BRAASCH

Right: Western red cedar (Thuja plicata). *Abundant rainfall and seasonal temperature moderated by the nearby ocean contribute to the factors that make Washington's coastal forests some of the temperate world's richest.* JEFF GNASS

Along the distant hills, a sharp line separates the lower slope from that above. A dusting of snow covers the trees above the line. Those below are the blue-green-gray of the coastal lowland. Like another shore, the snowline marks an upper limit to the coast country. Like a high-water mark, it reveals the extent of rain country—today's tenuous boundary with the whitened hilltops above. Among the lowland valleys, the land continually drinks the liquid that pours from the sky. And gives it back. It's a land of rivers, damp forests and bracken fern prairies where groundwater pours through porous gravel aquifers. Between its upper shore of snow, and its lower shore of saltwater, the lowland is a sea of swirling clouds, lingering fog, eddying rivers and lush forests. Water seems the common link, the process that unites all of the landscape and its living cover. Liquid courses through the pores of leaves, the vessels of root, trunk and bough. It churns through the veins of animals, mists in their breaths. It finds a million ways to pass through the land. To call coast country "dry" land is not quite correct.

The pioneer oceanographer Matthew Fontaine Maury once wrote: "Our planet is invested with two great oceans, one visible, the other invisible; one underfoot, the other overhead; one entirely envelops it, the other covers about two-thirds of its surface." Maury's powerful image of the unifying role of water was not intended for its figurative value—literally taken, it faithfully describes an elemental component of the earth's physical system. In coast country, that unity is apparent. Although the transition between sea and land may seem clear in the form of the shore, worlds on both sides of the breakers are worlds of water. The wave-scoured beach, the rain-scoured foothills and the glacier-scoured mountains are all products of Maury's various oceans. The living things, and especially the great coastal forest itself, can be considered water temporarily impounded in a vast reservoir of cells and tissues—a congealed sea.

Washington's coastal lowland, the band of country sandwiched above the tide and below the early-winter snow-

Cleahox Lake in Honeyman State Park near Florence. GEORGE WUERTHNER

line, represents the state's most productive and diverse habitat: forest canopies that blot out the sun, alder bottoms where twigs snap at the movement of deer and elk, streams that writhe with salmon, steelhead and cutthroat trout.

The most distinctive natural characteristic, and that which so thoroughly swallowed the first settlers of the coastal lowland, is its forest, its sea of trees that at one time extended from the water's edge into the mountain meadows. It is the proximity to the Pacific that creates the climate necessary to sustain such a sheer mass of greenery— the gently rising air currents shed their liquid load as the topography gently rises, the warm body of the nearby sea moderates seasonal temperature variation to within a comfortable range free from prolonged freezing or drought. Here the conifer reigns, able to withstand the dry summer months by holding moisture in its tough, wax-covered needle-leaves and continue producing sugar through the winter, when the broad-leaf trees are dormant.

Its original vastness and apparent uniformity notwithstanding, the forest is a complicated mix of individual forest communities; differences that characterize its patchwork composition are not visible until the eye has grown accustomed to the lay of the land, the subtle range of greens, the various forms, the microclimate preferences and the roles in succession that distinguish each species.

Nearest the coast, the forest is dominated by Sitka spruce, its distribution often associated with the summer fog belt. Spruce requires high humidity and can be found inland a considerable distance tucked deep in the wet valleys. On the Washington coast, this tree often exceeds 200' in height, its supple, strong and lightweight wood used formerly for airplane parts; now more commonly for musical instrument sounding boards. Spruce ranges nearly 2,000 miles along the Pacific Coast and in Washington it occupies the rain-choked valleys west of the Cascade summit as well as the coastal strip of the outer coast. Flagged and broken on coastal outcrops or straight and true in the protected rain-forest valleys, the blue-green cast of its bristly needles complements the even shade of mist that characterizes coast country.

Western red cedar is another familiar tree of the coast. Older trees—some as old as 1,000 years—often display forked, many-spired tops that rise above the surrounding forest canopy. Rot-resistant old-growth cedar has always been a particularly valuable forest resource. Material cultures of Native Americans were centered around the cedar tree, which provided shelter, clothing, canoes and innumerable other implements of survival. Anthropologists and botanists converge in theories that suggest that major climatic changes about 4,000 years ago brought about both the rise of the coastal cedar-hemlock forest and maritime tribal culture. The wood, light and easily fashioned by splitting or carving, was used in nearly every aspect of prehistoric life. White settlers, too, rapidly seized on the wood for split beams, puncheons, fenceposts and shakes.

Ironically, in country that fosters such luxuriant forest growth, cedar resources dwindle perilously because of the extended period required for cedar to develop the qualities that make it desirable as a wood. Second-growth red cedar grows too rapidly to develop the tight, straight grain that distinguishes old-growth wood. Further, it lacks the resistance to rot, which is found in old-growth—only a newcomer would use it for fenceposts. On the subject of the renewability of cedar resources, even the most progressive foresters remain mute, the hundreds of years required to produce high-quality wood are well beyond the planning horizon of the most enlightened forest manager.

In an undisturbed lowland forest, western hemlock is the most abundant tree. Its role in succession is that of a dominant species, so named because it can reproduce indefinitely in the darkened understory of the mature forest. All age-classes of western hemlock are present in the mature lowland forest, from minute seedlings bending out of their broken seed coverings and flimsy saplings rooted in rotted stumps, to tall adult trees piercing the forest canopy. Ecologically, hemlock represents the mature forest, where growth is offset by decay and the myriad interconnected ecological niches are occupied by a diverse flora and fauna. Because of its relative abundance, hemlock has grown in its importance as a forest product. It now far outranks Douglas fir as a common construction material and its fleecy fiber is a principal component of paper and cellulose products.

Douglas fir, owing to its aggressive "pioneering" habit and intolerance of shade as a seedling, occurs as the dominant tree form where disturbance has leveled the forest. According to Grays Harbor historian Edwin Van Syckle, evidence of a prehistoric coastal conflagration

Left: Horsetail and maple leaves. PAT O'HARA

Facing page: Sitka spruce (Picea sitchensis) occurs mainly within the coastal belt characterized by summer fog. These giants tower above 200' in the coastal rain forest. JEFF GNASS

Above: Forest carpet of wood sorrel, Oxalis oregana. ROBERT STEELQUIST
Right: Clearcutting duplicates the cycle of natural disturbance in the forest ecosystem, yet favors only a few tree species—those of high economic value. The long-term ecological implications of reducing forest diversity remain unknown. © GARY BRAASCH
Facing page: The Elwha River surges with a spring freshet. PAT O'HARA

that extended from the Columbia River to Ozette Lake suggests the reason that fir was so widespread in the lowland coastal region at the time of settlement. More recently, the "great" forest fires that burned about 26 square miles in the Grays Harbor region in 1902, and 35,000 acres in the Forks region in 1951, created broad Douglas fir forests. The "Great Blowdown" of 1921 leveled an estimated 2.5 million trees—it was estimated that one third of the trees in western Clallam County were flattened. Where fire and wind cut such wide swaths, Douglas fir returned in vast, even-aged stands of uniform boles.

On a smaller scale, Douglas fir is common along ridgetops where lightning strikes and wind play havoc with small patches of the forest giants. In an era of efficient fire-suppression methods, and of lowland forests made accessible by elaborate networks of logging roads, the "big burn" has become less likely. Nevertheless, the lowland forests of the Washington coast are far from fireproof. A 1978 wildfire started by lightning high on a ridge above the Hoh River Valley burned nearly 1,000 acres, descending in places to the Hoh River itself in the heart of the "rain forest." Within the span of a few years, life was again teeming in the Hoh burn.

Clearcut logging and the practices of silviculture that characterize the era of the "managed" forest have become the present-day equivalent of the massive fire and blowdown in determining that Douglas fir will dominate coastal timberlands. Modern practices perpetuate the cycle of disturbance and growth, on a 60-year rotation, that produces Douglas fir as nature produces it. What is gained is a steady flow of the preferred timber species to market. What is lost is the patchwork diversity of the coastal forest with all of its species, preferred and otherwise.

Disturbances by fire and windstorm are not the only factors that promote dramatic change in the coastal forest. In a region of superabundant rainfall, the work of rivers is itself mighty, and plays an important role in shaping forest composition. As alpine glaciers retreated into the mountains after the last Ice Age, they left behind broad, gravel-bottomed valleys, oversized for the rivers they now carry. As a result, rivers have considerable freedom to meander, carving new channels in the soft mantle of glacial overburden, altering their courses from one side to the other in the wide, relatively flat valleys. Coastal rivers have contributed explosive dynamism to the otherwise staid progression of growth and decay in the aged natural forests. With the onset of heavy winter rains, the rivers rise. As volume and velocity increase, the river has its way. It surges through the lowland, eating away gravel bluffs, laying new bars; toppling forest giants and heaping them in vast matchstick piles or transporting them to sea. Floodplains undergo vast redistribution of sediments. Where the water rises into a flat it lays a coat of fine sediments among the ferns and alders. Where it corners against a soft bluff, tons of debris are swept downstream. Boulders are heard in the torrent, thumping along the bottom; the water runs murky with particles of sand and clay.

The redistribution of material during the freshet creates new forest lands for alder, willow and cottonwood—hardwood species that line the riparian corridor. A fresh gravel bar can sprout a thicket of alder whips within weeks. Blackberry tendrils will reach into the open land during its first summer, fireweed and thistle capitalize on the openings as they do following a fire. In concert with the movement of the water itself, lowland valley forests respond quickly to every alteration of the riverbed terrain. Abandoned channels quickly fill with undergrowth and trees. In mature forests where the river has advanced into the understory, large forested areas can be undercut and carried away, allowing sunlight-loving trees to crowd into the new opening.

The development of the valley forest dramatically follows the development of the valley floor topography. Many river valleys display a series of terraces—old floodplain surfaces—that reflect the history of erosion and depo-

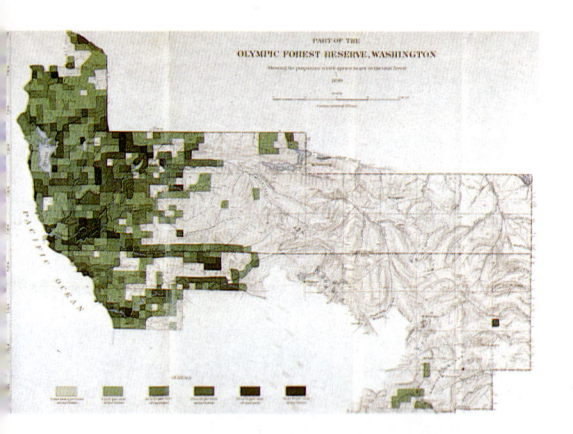

With the creation of the Olympic Forest Reserve in 1897, the wealth of Washington's coastal forest resources became known. Surveyors Arthur Dodwell and Theodore Rixon reported that the reserve contained America's richest stands of timber. KARNA ORSEN

River valleys consist of terraces composed of glacier- and river-laid gravel. Forest communities often correspond to particular river terraces, reflecting the stages of succession from the aggressive colonization of recently-disturbed terraces to the more stable mature forests of older terrace features. LAUREL BLACK

Facing page: No small amount of pride accompanied the conquering of the coastal forest primeval. Sharp steel and sharper reflexes were the faller's only advantages in his mission to harvest the forest bounty. HISTORICAL PHOTO COURTESY OF JONES PHOTO CO., ABERDEEN, WA

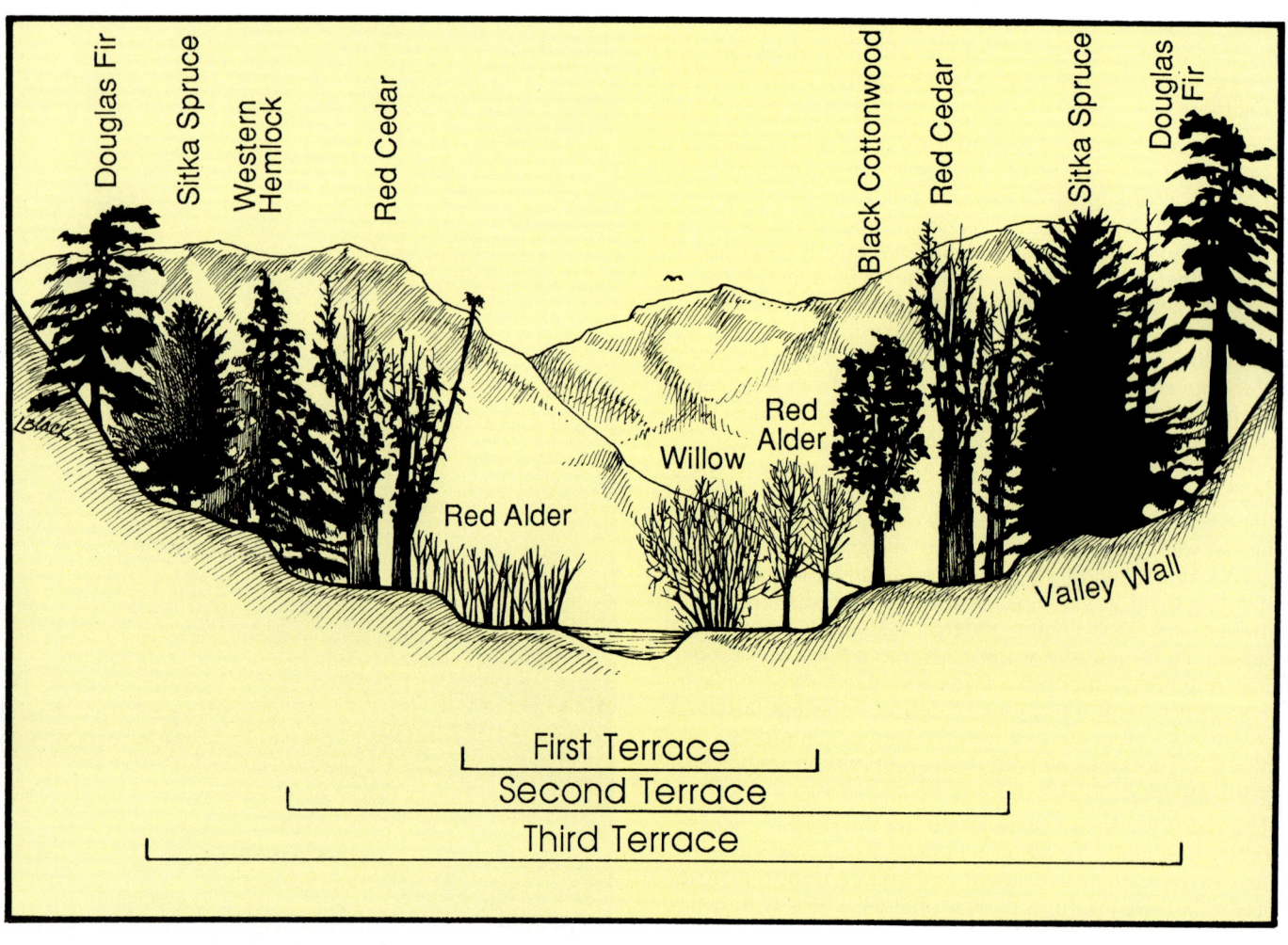

sition on the valley bottom over broad spans of time. Typically, the current floodplain, where water frequently covers the forest floor, will consist of fine particles and support alders, swordferns, salmonberry and grasses. Forest-floor wildflowers enjoy the early spring sunlight before the alder foliage closes the canopy. Away from the river, one, two, or as many as three, distinct, upper, old floodplain surfaces occur. Lower terraces may be dominated by young hemlock and cedar; higher terraces by mature cedar, hemlock and spruce. River-terrace forest composition reveals the elegant interplay between dynamic, living forest communities and the dynamic physi-

cal environment of coastal rivers. Each illustrates a play in the life-history of the river environment, with all of its physical, biological and ecological sub-plots.

For the most part, the great coastal forest yielded to settlement only after the water's front. Harbors were the first purchase that admitted Euro-American claimants. Places like Bruceport on Shoalwater Bay and New Dungeness were peopled in the 1850s. The backlands resisted intrusion until the mechanisms of taming the forests arrived on the scene. For the settler with a farming bent, the awful work of uncovering the soil was only a prelude, often unexpected, to the task of wresting a livelihood from the soil. Viewed as obstacles to farming rather than as valuable in and of themselves, giant trees were girdled to blanch their foliage and felled from bouncing springboards. Even after the fallen boles were burned or dragged away the looming forms of stumps crowded the new openings, giving rise to the early Northwest form of agriculture known as "stump farming."

Not only was farming difficult in the forested country of the coast, just getting around was a problem. So impenetrable was the country that in 1853, when Washington Territory was created, citizens of Shoalwater Bay felt far greater affinity to San Francisco, only a short ocean journey by schooner, than to Olympia, their territorial capital, a hundred miles away. In his book *Oysterville*, Willard Espy describes the overland journey to Olympia as so strenuous that Pacific County's first three delegates to the territorial legislature died from the labors of their travel before they could serve the good citizens of their district. The first wore himself out in the dense forest and managed to crawl back to his cabin, where he expired; the second was not so lucky—he passed on before he could crawl home; the third actually made it to Olympia and was sworn in, but died that night of apoplexy that the folks back home attributed to the travel. Water was the transportation network that served coastal settlements—the land was best left alone until the faller's axe, the crosscut saw, the ox and steam donkey created some breathing room so that one could actually see some part of the landscape. Eventually, the landscape emerged.

Once the owners or settlers of waterfront property (they were not always one-and-the-same) in the coastal region ran out of waterfront resources and started working on the woods themselves, Washington's coast became known for its timber. Lumber schooners regularly hauled bulging deckloads of sawn boards from early mills at Port Discovery, Port Angeles, Clallam Bay, Hoquiam, Aberdeen, Raymond and South Bend. Washington logs and lumber shored up the mines of Mexico and built (and rebuilt) many great cities where local timber was exhausted or nonexistent. It was the timber closest to tidewater that went first. Steep slopes that crowded the rivers, estuaries and the Strait of Juan de Fuca meant that trees could be felled directly into the water or dragged easily to the beach. At high tide they would be gathered and towed to the nearest mill.

Top: The relatively flat country of the Grays Harbor region yielded early to railroad logging. Polson Logging Co. employees pose in front of a Baldwin locomotive around the year 1910. HISTORICAL PHOTO COURTESY OF JONES PHOTO CO., ABERDEEN, WA
Above: Thick mats of club moss and fern adorn rainforest trees, creating a "second soil" laden with moisture and nutrients. Certain rainforest trees actually tap the living upholstery for nutrients. JEFF GNASS

As the shore was stripped, more creative methods were employed to move the logs to salt water. Splash dams could be constructed on many of the rivers, particularly those emptying into Grays Harbor. The Hoquiam, Humptulips, Wishkah and Wynooche watersheds all had numerous temporary impoundments where water was released in a surging artificial freshet, sending logs pouring through the valley toward saltwater. Despite problems of hang-ups, the uncertainty of ownership of logs mixed in the flood of jackstraws, and lawsuits by farmers whose land was badly eroded by the log drives, millions of board feet of timber reached the tidewater mills. The practice had its environmental consequences too—*Mountain in the Clouds* author Bruce Brown quoted a 1955 Washington Department of Fisheries study that reported that splash dams at one time blocked more than 60 percent of salmon streams with spawning or rearing potential in the Grays Harbor and Willapa Bay region.

By the time the timber was gone from the valley bottoms and steep canyons of the coastal tributaries, railroads had entered the country, ushering a new era into the land-clearing process. In *They Tried To Cut It All*, Edwin Van Syckle credits W.D. Mack with bringing the first steam locomotive to Grays Harbor country, in 1891. Railroad logging successfully penetrated much of the lowland coastal region. Van Syckle reports that a total of 1,095 miles of rail was laid in Grays Harbor country alone. Clallam County railroad historian Steve Hauff estimates the total mileage for the Northern Olympic Peninsula at about 500 miles and observes that technical progress in converting from ox to steam in the remote northern region lagged behind Grays Harbor by nearly a decade. Steam-driven iron shifted the balance in favor of the timbermen—the first third of the 20th century saw most of the lowland forests lost. In their place, a civilization of sorts had taken root. And what fragments we know today of the once-broad coastal tract of old-growth are those "locked up," to use the cliched plaint of those who would have cut it all.

While it was for some to exploit the coast's bountiful timber—to cut it, clear it and capitalize on it—it was for others to understand it, to comprehend the significance of one of the most productive natural communities of the temperate regions of the earth. Remnants of the undisturbed coast forest tell us a great deal about the subtle interplay of environmental factors with communities of living things. Fragments of valley rain forest preserved in the Olympic foothills in both Olympic National Park and Olympic National Forest reveal complex interactions of nutrient flow through the ecosystem. Although Olympic National Park was formed primarily to protect elk herds, the recognition of the importance of rain forest as winter habitat had the additional benefit preserving forest processes themselves. The study of those forests has led to significant discoveries that aid in understanding temperate and tropical forests as whole ecosystems that are becoming critically necessary.

In studies conducted in the rain forest of the Hoh River Valley, beginning in about 1980, researcher Nalini Nadkarni made a startling discovery. She found that several species of moss-festooned hardwood—bigleaf maple, vine maple and red alder—took advantage of their dense mats of encrusting moss, club-moss, liverworts and lichens by sending roots into the bulging masses of epiphytes *(epi,* "upon"; *phyte,* "plant")* that cling picturesquely to the trees' boughs and trunks. Previously, such masses of extraneous plant material clinging to tree trunks and limbs in the rain forest were thought to be of little or no ecological significance to the forest. Nadkarni's discovery, however, revealed that there was some mechanism of interdependence between the trees and their upholstery. Her conclusion was that the roots extending out of the upper boughs and trunks of the trees and into the epiphytic mats were actually drawing moisture and nutrients from the bundles, which are very efficient at trapping moisture and nutrients from rainwater, mist and wind-blown dust. By weighing the epiphyte masses from individual trees, she calculated that epiphytes alone weighed 6,000 pounds per acre, or about four times the weight of the foliage of the trees they lived upon. Taken as a whole, the living garlands contributed enormously to the reservoir of nutrients available to the trees of the rain forest. This becomes even more significant in view of the fact that rain forest soils are rather low in soil nutrients due to excessive leaching in areas where annual rainfall often exceeds 150".

Nadkarni persisted in her study of what she termed "canopy rooting." Her subsequent studies in tropical forests around the world have confirmed that aerial roots that penetrate epiphyte mats form an adaptation that has evolved separately in scores of tree species, many of which are taxonomically very remote. Such a mechanism, she observed, allows rain forest trees to take a "short cut" in obtaining nutrients in short supply in the forest ecosystem, by capturing the nutrients before they filter down into the soil where other plant forms can use them.

The impending loss of old-growth forest resources throughout the Pacific Northwest led to an important series of studies to understand precisely what mechanisms are at work in old-growth forests, but are absent in younger forests and those under intense management for timber production. Significant among the conclusions was the fundamental concept—long misunderstood—that forest soils of the coast region are not rich in nutrients. Clearly it is difficult to conceive that lush forest, capable of overgrowing a derelict homestead in decades, does not spring from rich soil. Instead, it is the abundance of organic material—dead and alive—from which forest life springs, and nutrients are captured, held and recycled.

Old-growth forests are defined as those typically between 350 and 750 years of age, west of the Cascades and dominated by western hemlock, although Douglas fir also may occur in the mature forest. At this age, wood is gradually being added to the stand although at a rate that is significantly lower than in a younger stand. Among the most significant characteristics of the old-growth forest is the amount of decayed and decaying material both in standing snags and as fallen logs on the ground.

Because of the complex structure and niche variety unique to the old-growth forest, numerous species of birds and mammals find the mature forests optimum habitat; some are found only in the dwindling stands of old-growth. Birds dependent on old-growth for nesting include the spotted owl, goshawk, and Vaux's swift. Mammals that rely heavily on old-growth include marten, fisher, northern flying squirrel, red tree vole and silver-haired bat, among others. Others too find that old-growth is ideal for feeding and shelter, among them the brightly crested and raucous pileated woodpecker, which plunders carpenter ants.

In addition to providing substantial niches for cavity nesters, insects and insect-eaters, the presence of decaying organic litter supports large quantities of nitrogen-fixing bacteria that add greatly to the nutrient reservoir "locked" in the forest. In addition, phosphorus and calcium increase significantly through the decomposition of downed logs. As a result of these processes, old-growth forests retain and enhance soil nutrients otherwise lost because of soil leaching in areas of heavy precipitation.

The presence of "nurse logs"—decomposing logs that sport a thick coat of spruce, hemlock and cedar seedlings—also attests to the importance of large woody organic debris on the forest floor. Large quantities of moisture are retained in the rotting material, which, along

Top: Decks loaded, the lumber schooner Edward R. West *awaits departure from Grays Harbor. Photo circa 1920.* WILLIAM D. JONES HISTORICAL COLLECTION, COURTESY OF JONES PHOTO CO., ABERDEEN, WA

Above: Insects are a critical link between the plant and animal domains of the forest. CINDY McINTYRE

33

Top: Old growth. TOM & PAT LEESON
Above: Blacktail deer (Odoccileus hemionus). KEITH D. LAZELLE

Facing page: The Cedar Grove on Long Island, Willapa Bay, may have remained undisturbed for as long as 4,000 years—a rare fragment of natural antiquity. © GARY BRAASCH

with nutrients, make the logs a perfect rooting medium for the tiny plants. Scientists have noticed, in contrast, that pastures and cultivated fields of old homesteads, where exposed mineral soil and abundant sunlight would suggest that seedlings should prosper, remain devoid of large numbers of conifer seedlings. While evergreen seedlings sprout vigorously from nearby stumps and logs, bare ground supports only grasses and disturbance–loving shrubs. The healing of such places, the restoration of the proper amounts of forest litter and woody debris, may require centuries.

The 1984 "discovery" of a minute parcel of elegantly grotesque and archaic cedars and hemlocks took forest ecologists by total surprise. Located on 5,000-acre Long Island in Willapa Bay, "The Cedar Grove" consists of 274 acres of ancient cedars and hemlocks. The cedars range from 8' to 11' in diameter, their bleached and forked tops pierce the surrounding forest canopy 150' above the dark forest floor. Some are estimated to be 1,000 years old. The presence of the stand was well known to a few naturalists, and local managers of both Willapa National Wildlife Refuge and Weyerhaeuser Company—each an owner of a portion of the grove. What was not known about this particular stand of trees, is that as a community, the grove appears to have escaped disturbance—natural or man-caused—for at least 2,000 and perhaps 4,000 years. Wildfire, windstorm and flood, the natural forces that periodically and catastrophically destroy mature forests and begin the process of succession anew, had never overcome the tiny island enclave. And, even more miraculously, the forest went untouched by loggers during the 130-year period since settlement—a period that saw most of the coastal forest logged at least twice.

In terms of the theory of forest succession—the process by which a series of plant species dominate the community following a disturbance—the "climax" state was originally conceived as the stage at which the forest reaches its peak of structural complexity, and compositional and energetic stability. In the words of pioneer plant ecologist Frederic E. Clements, "Each formation [climax community] is the highest type of vegetation possible under its particular climate, and this relation makes the term climax especially significant, as it is derived from the same root as climate."

In Clements' model, devised around the turn of the century, plant communities advance from a state of imbalance following a disturbance, to a state of perfect balance, an organic unfolding of an ultimate refinement between organism and environment. "Each climax is the direct expression of its climate; the climate is the cause, the climax the effect, which, in its turn, reacts upon the climate," he wrote. Modern ecologists credit Clements with creating a powerful model for interpreting change in natural systems but disagree that the process builds an idealized state of natural perfection—the consumate fit, the biological Utopia.

Jan Henderson, a forest ecologist for the U.S. Forest Service, says "We don't hold on to the underlying belief that Clements used, that changes must lead to some ultimate state. Landscapes and natural systems are the way they are; ideas are interpretations of things, not the things themselves."

To Henderson and other ecologists, another problem plagued such an ideal arrangement: it had never been found in a coastal forest community. The development of a climax in Clements' terms takes so long, and disturbance is such a common occurrence in a region of wind, water, summer drought and lightning, that the millenia required for a climax to form would probably also see major climatic changes, as have indeed been revealed in higher-elevation forest communities. Nevertheless, much to their astonishment, on Long Island forest ecologists think they found one—a confirmation of an entity predicted in theory, but perhaps not previously recognized.

Many very old forest communities are known in coast country, though only on sites under stringent protective management. But each bears the scar of some natural catastrophe that, in the relatively recent past, has upset the cycle and deflected the process back to an earlier stage. On Long Island, cedars and their hemlock cohorts have survived natural ravages for up to perhaps 4,000 years as a coherent unit. Henderson thinks that their proximity to the moderating influence of the Pacific may have insulated them from changes of the climate that are evidenced by fluctuations in alpine glacial systems and responses by other forest communities. In the dampness of the lowland, sheltered from catastrophic fire by the moat of Willapa Bay, protected from windstorm blasts by their own tight ranks, the age-old trees have persisted despite extraordinary odds.

Their value is debated—not as a fact, but from various perspectives. For Weyerhaeuser Company accountants, the trees are assets for which the federal government had better compensate them richly (above current market rates, they say); for the U.S. Fish and Wildlife Service, they form a unique habitat (spotted owls have been seen on the site) that complements the diversity of Willapa National Wildlife Refuge. For others, including Henderson, they are remarkable evidence of the complex dynamism at work in plant communities that endure the ages. To a few who know them, they are the balance of a once-vast inheritance that was spent—sometimes in innocence and sometimes in recklessness—in a few hurly-burly generations. Literally and symbolically, the 274 acres are the climax—of nearly 150 years of the opening of a dark and forested land; of perhaps 4,000 years of the life of a forest that is literally the living substance of both oceans of the coast.

Upon this land a great sea washes. It boils gray onto the rocks and bursts white; it vaporizes. It rolls over the plain in dark, brooding mists. It pours in torrents as rain. It floods the valleys with dull, colored runoff. In ancient gnarled boughs and rotted stumps and in tender needles it takes refuge. On the distant hills it leaves its finely powdered spindrift—the line marked by fresh snowfall.

OIL CITY

During the winter of 1906-1907, surveyors discovered an oil seep beneath a large stump in the vicinity of Hoh Head, just north of the mouth of the Hoh River. It was not a startling discovery—oil seeps had been reported in several locations along the Washington Coast. Local Indians had known of several seeps; they called sandy clay found around them "smell mud."

The Hoh Head seep attracted little more than curiosity until 1911, when several young men dynamited the adjacent rocks, allowing the oil to flow into a pit where it could be collected by dipping. Once a small sample had been taken interest perked up. By 1913, the Jefferson Oil Company had been formed and a prospect pit 18 feet deep had been dug at the seep. In July of 1913, tons of equipment were brought by barge to Jefferson Cove, just south of Hoh Head, and ferried through the surf onto the beach. A steam donkey winched the machinery up the cliff face and inland to the site of the oil seep.

On September 10, 1913, the Jefferson Oil Company began drilling in earnest, using a 72-foot derrick rig. In October, Charles T. Lupton visited the site, in order to prepare a report for the United States Geological Survey. At the time of his visit, the Jefferson Oil Company well was 445 feet deep and according to the author "gas was escaping from the well in small volume, as shown by the bubbling of water in the casing. There was also a slight trace of oil in the material brought to the surface by the bailer from the bottom of the hole." Under close scrutiny, the oil was green in color and smelled "like Pennsylvania oil." Laboratory analysis gave it a specific gravity of 0.8679, with a boiling point of 103 degrees Celsius. The oil was characterized as high grade, with a paraffin base.

Natural oil seeps near the mouth of the Hoh River fueled hopes of fortune for drillers during the early 1900s and again during the 1930s. Here a Hoh Oil Co. derrick stands above one of the company's several unsuccessful holes, circa 1935. COURTESY OF JONES PHOTO CO., ABERDEEN, WA

The well reached 868 feet in depth in early 1914. The driller's log revealed interbedded layers of shale, sand, clay and sandstone. In spite of the heroic effort needed to develop the isolated site and the promising shows of petroleum, the well was abandoned because commercial quantities were not forthcoming.

Drilling near Hoh Head resumed in the 1930s, when the Leslie Oil Co. and the Washington Oil Co. Ltd. established several more test holes near the old oil seep. One hole, the Kipling No. 1, had the distinction of being Washington's first oil well that went into production. The well was started on April 5, 1936, struck oil at 287 feet and was completed on May 10, at a total depth of 314 feet. According to a report by Sheldon L. Glover, a geologist for the State of Washington, "in the 12 hours following completion, oil rose 114 feet in the six-inch casing. On May 11, 1936, the well was placed on the pump and the available storage, a 50-barrel tank, was partially filled by the small pump at the rate of approximately 3½ barrels per hour."

Glover was optimistic for the future of the wells in the vicinity. Eventually, 11 test wells were drilled. Glover's hopes were shared by others, who, smelling the sweet aroma of petroleum, also smelled commercial opportunity. Eager developers platted the townsite of Oil City, about two miles from the well site. Shacks were constructed for the workers and a plank roadway built to the wells. The expected boom, however, fizzled. Producing wells soon slowed to a trickle. When the aromatic green petroleum yielded no fortunes, it was clear that Oil City would not live up to either part of its name.

In time, it was the green of the forest that dominated Oil City. Thickets of salal overtook the well sites, weathered shacks collapsed, and abandoned machinery rusted silently. The oil, what little there is, remains, although the site is now located in Olympic National Park. "Smell mud" still gives off its odor and volatile bubbles still rise in the abandoned casings.

There is a genuine mud volcano on our property and we are drilling the well on the side of the cone of this gas-vent. Newburger & Noalhat, the great Galician authorities,... say: "Mud volcanoes are always a sure sign of petroleum in the subjacent strata of the neighborhood." Cunningham-Craig, great English authority, in "Oil Finding,"... says that where there is a mud volcano "there is no doubt as to the presence of oil beneath the surface."

A lot of people have been wondering why W.H. Paulhamus, who has done so much for the actual development of Western Washington, and E.F. Gregory, who has done so much in the development of the City of Tacoma, have gone into a company prospecting for oil. The answer is that they have been foremost in other kinds of development and they are taking part in the development of oil for the same progressive reason.

"I believe that the stock of this company will be worth $100 a share within a reasonably short time. This belief is the reason I am identified with this company."—E.F. Gregory

"I am positive that the showing of oil on the property of the Queniult Oil Company is the greatest showing of oil ever found in North America."—J.A. Paulhamus.

...Congressman Albert Johnson, who returned to Tacoma after a visit...declared that he had no doubt that the oil was there and it was only a question of time before it would be discovered. "We had a fine trip...I am much interested in the oil situation. While I was unable to visit the wells that are now being sunk, I feel sure that oil is there and that it probably lies in a large lake somewhere on the peninsula. It is merely a question of hitting the right spot."

"There is no chance of striking oil in this state," declares a friend of yours. That was the same cry in Texas, and California, and Wyoming, and Utah, and Pennsylvania, and every place else, before they struck oil.

From Queniult Oil Co. stock prospectus, 1914.
WASHINGTON STATE HISTORICAL SOCIETY

CHAPTER THREE

LIFE OF THE COAST

KARNA ORSEN

Sanderlings (Crocethia alba) *drill the wet sand, capitalizing on the biological richness of the shore—the ultimate edge.* FRANK S. BALTHIS

The study of sea life is at once as ancient as man and as fresh as each day's discovery. Aristotle made observations on sea-life that would credit even trained contemporary observers. Nevertheless, at the frontiers of marine biology, new questions arise as quickly as old ones are answered. The vastness and complexity of the marine ecosystem, and its inhospitable nature as a laboratory, keep researchers focused on organisms and technologies with direct applicability to society. As a result, marine resources like salmon are relatively well understood, while life-histories of many fishes and most invertebrates remain life-mysteries. There are even whale species about which science knows next to nothing. Discoveries being made at marine biology's cutting edge jostle our assumptions and cause us to reorder our neat divisions of the living world by showing us exception after exception to the rules.

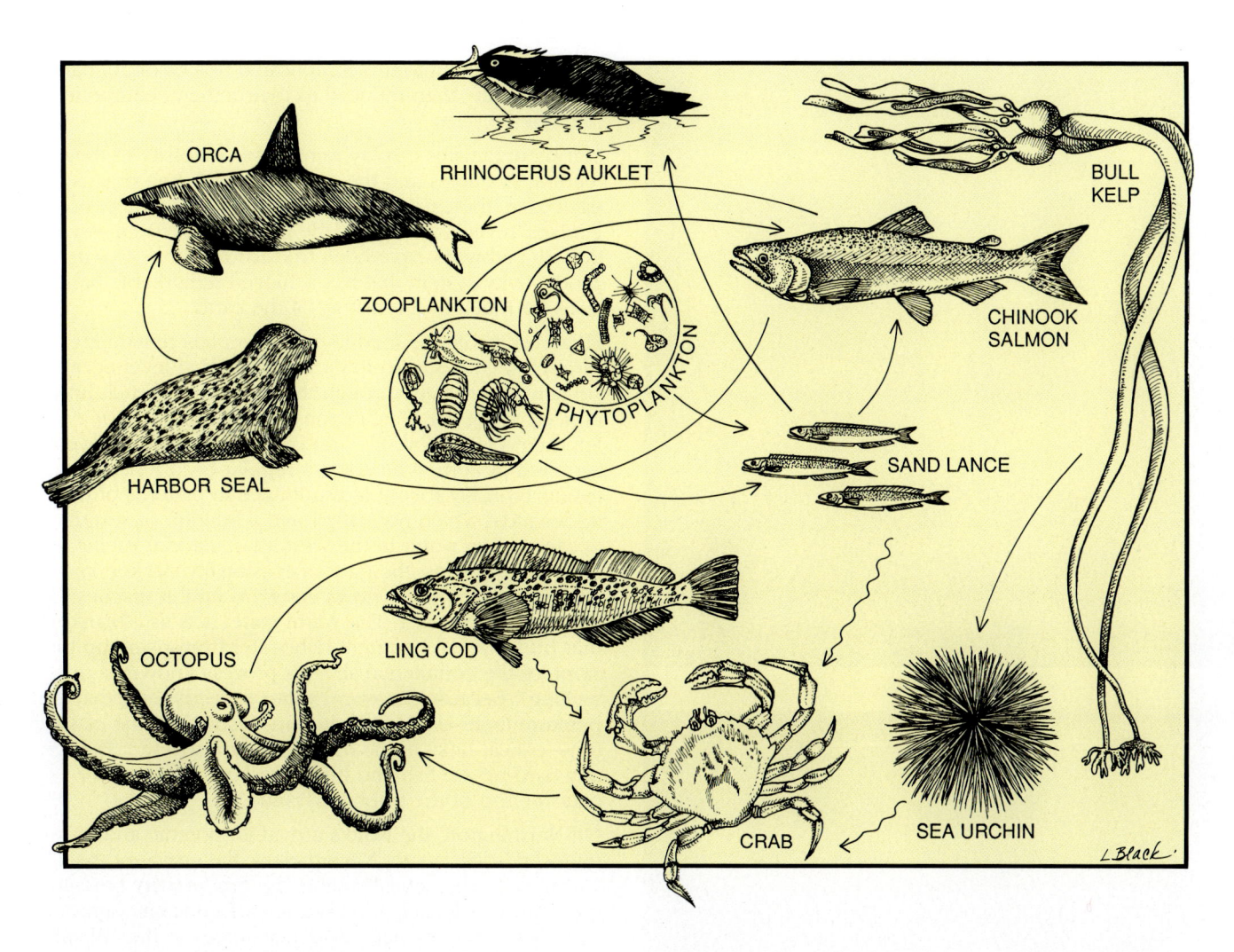

The sea's phenomenal ability to convert solar energy into living organisms supports its complicated chains of life. Based on a potent alchemy of sunlight, water temperature, the presence of nutrients and photosynthesis in marine algae, the productivity cycle supports some of the tiniest organisms known, as well as the largest. Marine food webs, like those of terrestrial communities, are composed of interconnecting pathways that link each organism to the whole.

Food webs are seen as a series of trophic levels, each characterized by the general nature of the transfer of food energy. Algae and plants capable of producing food energy through photosynthesis are called autotrophic, ("self-feeding"); organisms that must consume other organisms to obtain nutrients are said to be heterotrophic. Food webs are further organized into groups of organisms named for their principal food source: herbivores eat plant materials; piscivores eat fishes; carnivores eat meat; scavengers are opportunistic feeders that feed on organic detritus. Taken as a whole, there is tremendous conservation in such a complex and many-tiered system—the leftovers of one organism's lunch are the ingredients of another's dinner. Organic substances

Left: Life of the coast is interconnected in complex food chains consisting of plant organisms that convert sunlight to food energy, herbivores that thrive on the plant materials, predators that feed on other animal forms and scavengers that recycle organic debris. LAUREL BLACK *Top:* The sea's edge is a lush expression of life's diversity. In the rocky intertidal zone, competition for space is a fact of life. *Bottom:* Sea-palm forests thrive in the middle intertidal zone.
TIM THOMPSON PHOTOS

Coho smolts—newly silvered following their migration to salt water—feed in estuaries and nearshore areas before embarking on their long ocean journeys. TIM THOMPSON

An outbreak of the parasite "N.I.X." (Nuclear Inclusion X) clouds the future of the razor clam sport fishery. Appearing during the 1982-83 El Niño, its cause remains uncertain. BOB & IRA SPRING

are constructed into the complicated tissues of animal and plant life, then reduced to their mineral components in endless cycles.

Marine organisms display remarkable diversity in their feeding strategies and the anatomy of feeding organs. In each case, the extreme specialization seen in most organisms reveals the age of the marine ecosystem—evolutionary pathways have been trod for millions of years in a productivity system that has achieved remarkable balance for much of the history of the earth.

However stable the marine ecosystem has remained through the ages, disturbances on a global level occasionally reverberate through the system. One such upset noticed along the Washington coast is the El Niño/Southern Oscillation. El Niño is the name that the event acquired in Peru, where it is a regular occurrence. Niño events typically follow a disturbance in patterns of the tradewinds, which normally force a buildup of warmer ocean surface water in the western equatorial Pacific. For unknown reasons, the trades occasionally slacken and the warmer surface water flows eastward until it reaches the South America coast. The warm water acts as a blanket that prevents cold nutrient-rich water from rising up the slope of the continental shelf (a process known as upwelling). Because the warm water exceeds the lethal temperature limits of many organism—especially the plankton—critical links in the food chain are severed. Especially hard-hit are fish and bird populations that thrive near the top of the trophic pyramid.

Off Washington, the Niño's arrival is sporadic and its intensity is less acute. Nevertheless, the arrival of the warm water dramatically alters the productivity scheme of the Northeast Pacific and critically affects many organisms. The most dramatic evidence comes in the appearance of exotic pelagic (ocean-roaming) life-forms—fishes and seabirds usually not seen as far north as our shore, and unusual behavior patterns in those that regularly inhabit our waters.

During the 1982-83 El Niño, northerly range extensions were established for finescale triggerfish, prickly shark, spotted cusk-eel, swordfish and popeye catalufa. In addition, fishes that have made rare appearances here—including hammerhead sharks, blue sharks, jack mackerel, swordfish, barracuda, white seabass and others—made return visits. Leatherback turtles were reported from several Washington coastal sites as were brown pelicans (some observers note that pelicans have become more regular visitors since the 1982-83 Niño event). Washington appearances were made by magnificent frigatebirds and Caspian and elegant terns.

Dramatic behavioral changes were seen in albacore tuna, which moved closer to shore as the warm water disrupted the warm- and cold-water boundary where they ordinarily school. Several salmon species altered their migratory patterns to avoid the flood of warm water. In addition, fur seal herds that roam the northeast Pacific searching for salmon and other prey displayed more aggressive behavior, a clue to some observers that hunger was taking its toll.

The food web of the northeast Pacific includes people. Great economic significance is given to the status of marine resources that feed us and that feed coastal communities thriving on the ocean's bounty. The El Niño of 1982-83 awakened many to the necessary dependency that even we, land-bound, air-breathing bipeds, have upon the physical and biological events that resonate through the sea.

Living Communities of the Coast

At sea, biological evidence suggests the nearness of a shore, even when the highest peaks have disappeared off the rolling horizon to the east. Land-nesting storm petrels pluck tiny fish and shrimp from the surface layer of saltwater; gulls raucously dive for meaty scraps thrown overboard from fishing vessels; puffins fly past like kamikaze circus clowns—their brilliant, oversized beaks being chased by their unlikely bird-bodies.

Continental shelf sediments are a rich store of nutrients, leached from the land and accumulated as the detritus of the complex web of life. In the relative shallows, sunlight has full play, blooming the suspended gardens of drifting phytoplankton *(phyto,* "plant"; *plankton,* "drifting")— diatoms and blue-green algae. It is the physical process of upwelling that blends the sediment-nutrients with the hanging garden of life in the sunlit upper water. Although upwelling regions comprise only one-tenth of a percent of the world's ocean area, they produce more than 44 percent of the world's fish.

Upwelling contributes significantly to the life of the Northwest coast, although the textbook examples of it are found elsewhere, such as the western coasts of Peru and Equa-

Brown pelicans (Pelicanus occidentalis) *are seen more commonly along parts of the Washington Coast following a sudden appearance associated with the 1982-83 El Niño.*

Tufted puffin (Lunda cirrhata). JEFF FOOTT PHOTOS

dor. In Washington, upwelling occurs during the summer months when high-pressure systems push the wind southward along the coast. Such winds, coupled with the rotation of the earth, have the effect of forcing surface seawater offshore, and drawing colder bottom water upward to take its place. The reaction is profound. Large quantities of bottom nutrients are fed into the sunlight zone, producing a seasonal burst of plant plankton, the foundation of the food pyramid.

Pelagic life-forms benefit strongly from upwelling. These include ocean-roamers like finback and blue whales that strain the water through their sieves of baleen for the rich, drifting clouds of zooplankton (*zoo,* "animal"; *plankton,* "drifting") that feed on the suspended vegetable particles. Other pelagic forms include tuna, Pacific Ocean perch and the vast shoals of salmon caught up in the circular motion of their migration and not yet sorted into their respective cohort groups of river-brothers and -sisters. Whole navies of *Velella velella,* By-the-wind-sailors, ply the main with transparent sails aloft. These tiny relatives of jellyfish, along with true jellyfish, are the food of the disc-like ocean sunfish, a pelagic wanderer that reaches 10' in length and resembles a giant head.

The Kelp Forest

Closer to shore, life-forms take on more familiar forms. Kelp beds are the marine equivalent of the coastal rain forest, an observation made by Charles Darwin in 1834. Lush expressions of vegetative extravagance, they form habitats of great structural complexity that shelter a host of marine organisms. Darwin, upon seeing luxuriant kelp growth in the Strait of Magellan, wrote: "The number of living creatures of all Orders, whose existence intimately depends on the kelp, is wonderful. A great volume might be written, describing the inhabitants of one of these beds of sea-weed."

Two species of brown algae form the dominant members of the kelp community on Washington's coast—one, bull kelp *(Nereocystis leutkeana),* in the relatively protected waters of the Strait and outer coast; the other, perennial kelp *(Macrocystis integrifolia),* on the exposed outer coast with its heavier wave action. Both species thrive on rocky substrate and occur in dense patches where water depth does not exceed 30' to 40'. Both species attach to the bottom with holdfasts, clusters of tentacle-like projections that grow around rocks and other objects and anchor the plant. Both plants also consist of long stipes, stem-like gas-filled tubes that sometimes reach 40' in length. The blades are attached differently. On perennial kelp, one blade will project from each float; many floats grow from a single stipe, spaced along the stipe at even intervals of several inches. On bull kelp, stipes terminate in one large float, with several blades attached to the float. In both species, the floats support the blades at the surface of the water, where photosynthesis can take place. Like the giant trees of the terrestrial rain forest, kelp plants often support "rugs" of epiphytic algae on their floats and upper stipes.

Vertebrate animals that inhabit kelp beds include mammals and fishes that find food and shelter among the floating forests. Sea otters are highly dependent upon kelp beds. Sea urchins, which graze on kelp, are a dietary staple for the sleek mammals. In addition, otters are frequently observed sleeping in the dense tangles and they seek the shelter of the wave-damping beds during violent storms. Protective mothers have been observed winding kelp around the leg of a baby; the kelp "babysitter" secures the pup while the mother forages.

The green world of filtered light and dangling stalks offers a maze of passages and escapes for fishes. Lingcod, kelp greenling, various perch species, cabezon, several rockfish species, wolf eel and red Irish lord are significant larger fish species; larval rockfish, sticklebacks, penpoint gunnels and tubesnouts are smaller species regularly inhabiting the floating forests. Invertebrates include amphipods, copepods, isopods, euphasids, numerous species of crab, and shrimp. Structurally and ecologically, kelp forests form important habitat in nearshore waters.

Left: Two species of kelp form most of Washington's rich kelp habitats: Bull kelp (Nereocystis luetkeana), *with its single float and long stipe; and giant kelp* (Macrocystis integrifolia), *with its numerous floats and wrinkled blades.* TIM THOMPSON

Above: Thick beds of kelp provide a complex habitat that benefits hundreds of other species by providing food and shelter and by cushioning wave action. JEFF FOOTT

Facing page: By-the-wind-sailors (Velella velella), *pelagic roamers that drift before the sea wind.* KEITH D. LAZELLE

The intertidal zone—a world between worlds. Life-forms array themselves in horizontal bands that correspond to a whole range of physical and biological factors. Wave intensity, predation and tolerance to drying are just a few. DOUG WECHSLER

The Rocky Intertidal

The world of the rocky intertidal zone is actually two worlds: a land world exposed when the tide is out, an ocean world when the tide is in. Plants and animals that live here must be able to survive the extremes of freezing winter weather and scalding summer sun as well as the fury of exploding waves. Many animals, like barnacles and mussels, that are exposed at low tide become inactive, closing their shells and withdrawing their gills and mouthparts. Other intertidal animals, such as shore crabs and rock crabs, crawl under rocks or seaweed and wait for the tide to return. Sea anemones retract their soft tentacles and appear as inconspicuous jelly-like buds. In tidepools, sculpins and other fishes seek cover amid the sand and cobbles, the camouflage of their varied markings helping to make them inconspicuous.

The period during which intertidal organisms are exposed is also for them a period of quiet. Reduced activity also reduces their need for oxygen, which for gill-breathing animals is in short supply while the tide is out. When oxygen-rich water again surrounds them, they resume movement and feeding activity. Also, at low tide, exposed animals are extremely vulnerable to gulls and other predators that forage actively among tidepools and colonies of barnacles and mussels—remaining inconspicuous is one way to avoid being eaten.

What is immediately apparent about a rocky intertidal community is a pattern of distinct bands or zones of animal and plant communities. These bands correspond to wave-action intensity at different tide levels, tolerances of certain types of animals for exposure to air and sunlight and the presence or absence of certain predators. Intertidal zonation has been the object of much study, and various systems have been applied depending on locality and investigator. Typically, however, zone systems consist of a splash zone, and upper, middle and lower intertidal zones.

The splash zone is the highest layer of marine life in the layer-cake pattern of the intertidal zone. It is also the most sparsely populated. This area is flooded only during intense storms and by the spray of surf when the tide is high. Its occupants include limpets, periwinkles, occasional acorn barnacles, pale-green sea hair (an algae) and black encrusting lichens. The upper intertidal area is flooded during normal high tides. Here, acorn and thatched barnacles are abundant, along with limpets, black turban snails and mussels. Seaweeds, such as rockweed (with little air sacs) and sea lettuce (pale green, translucent sheets), are present. Hermit crabs and shore crabs occupy this zone. In tidepools of this zone, look for tidepool sculpins, broad-headed fish with dark, saddle-like bars across the back.

The middle intertidal contains more animals than the higher zones and remains submerged for longer periods of time. In this zone, mussels grow profusely. Edible blue mussels are common here, as well as ochre sea stars (some are orange, some purple). These sea stars are the most important predators of the intertidal zone—it is their presence that determines the lower boundary for mussel communities. Living among the mussel colonies are limpets, snails, worms and small crabs. Black chitons and whelks are also common here. In tidepools of the middle intertidal zone, surf grass often grows in sand-filled pockets between the boulders, and magenta coral-leaf alga forms vivid splashes over rocks and many relatively sedentary organisms including rock scallops and dunce-cap limpets.

The lower intertidal zone is uncovered only during the lowest tides and is home to hundreds of species of animals and plants. At very low tides, pools and channels are exposed, sometimes trapping subtidal life forms like the wolf eel and octopus. Green sea anemones, purple and red sea urchins, orange sea cucumbers, opalescent nudibranchs and a host of other brightly colored organisms crowd together in this zone.

The Sandy Intertidal

Not all intertidal habitats reveal their inhabitants in such gaudy splendor as the rocky shore. On broad, sandy, wave-swept expanses of beach, organisms burrow deep into the sediments to wait out the ebb. The razor clam can burrow quickly, forcing its foot into the sand, expanding the tip, then contracting the foot muscle to pull itself deeper. Razor clam populations once were the principal tourist draw to the sandy beaches of the southern Washington coast, have fallen on hard times since outbreaks of a lethal disorder known as "Nuclear Inclusion X." The disease is thought to have been associated with the 1982-83 El Niño. Resource managers keep a watchful eye on razor clam populations, optimistic that a rebound will occur.

Spatial arrangements of intertidal communities reflect both competition for surface area and specific environmental tolerances of organisms. Bare spots, caused by wave-thrown logs and other debris, are usually recolonized quickly. PAT O'HARA

Bottom fishes such as the C-O sole (Pleuronichtys coenosus) *are naturally adapted to sandy habitats. Concealment mechanisms such as flat body form, protruding eyes and variable skin pigmentation enable them to conceal themselves in and on the sand bottom.* LEO J. SHAW, COURTESY THE SEATTLE AQUARIUM

Dungeness crabs also forage the sandy intertidal, retreating with the water when possible, seeking the shelter of kelp or burrowing into the sand when retreat is precluded. Dungeness crabs are predators of clams but scavenge most of their food. The sand-dollar requires sandy bottom for its survival. Sand dollars are close relatives of sea urchins; living specimens are covered with bristly hairs, anatomic counterparts of the tube-feet and spines of sea urchins, and inhabit sandy beds standing on edge and leaning with the current, feeding on fine bits of detritus that they pass from tube-foot to tube-foot and place in their mouths. Snails of the sandy intertidal include the Lewis moon snail, which can attain the size of a baseball, and the diminutive purple olive snail. Both snails plow through the sand, often completely buried, in their search for food.

Sandy beaches are also home to beach hoppers. Millions of these isopods occupy the line of drift strewn along the beach at high tide where they feed on decomposing organic material. Their presence alerts us to the wide variety of smaller invertebrates that inhabit the sand. Vast populations of tiny crustaceans burrow in the sand and attract the large flocks of shorebirds that scurry along the water's foaming edge, plucking live morsels from the damp sand.

As the tide floods over the broad beach, bottom fishes return with it. Flounder and sole weather the turbid environment in which each passing wave stirs a submarine sandstorm. These flatfish bury themselves in the loose substrate, settling into the bottom with writhing motions that stir the sediments around them. Mechanisms in the nervous system enable them to concentrate or disperse color pigments in their skin to match the color of their surroundings. Bulging eyes are frequently the only visible signs of a flounder's presence as it rests on the bottom.

Redtail, calico and silver surfperch also follow the water's edge and are among the principal fish species caught by surf anglers. The sand lance is an important forage fish that inhabits the sandy bottom. When alarmed, these long silver fish dart into the sand, slithering to shelter head-first.

Cobble Beaches

Cobble beaches are common along the relatively protected Strait of Juan de Fuca and on protected coves of the outer coast where glacial outwash and till blanket the uplands. Cobble beaches support a much greater diversity of organisms than sand because of the increased size of cavities between individual rocks. The wealth of the cobble beach is its hardshell clams—common species of the Strait include the horse clam; the butter, or Washington, clam; the native littleneck; the Japanese littleneck or Manila clam; and the heart cockle. Specific habitats of the clams vary: some prefer larger or smaller substrate than the others and each has its own vertical station of the beach where it thrives. Productivity on cobble beaches can be phenomenal—one littleneck grower reported beds that produced well more than a cubic foot of clams in a cubic foot of substrate. Only thinning the clams at an immature stage allowed adequate growing room for the remainder.

Native littlenecks remaining in Sequim and Discovery bays on the Strait of Juan de Fuca represent the majority of commercially viable populations remaining in Puget Sound. Sedimentation and other water-quality problems have eliminated the natives from much of their original range. Although the introduction of the more tolerant Manila clam has provided growers with a hardy substitute, the exotic lacks some of the delicate eating qualities of the native and has provided a convenient dodge from serious water-quality questions that the native's disappearance raised.

The Estuary

Where coastal rivers enter the sea occurs a netherworld of fresh- and saltwater habitats, known as the estuary. Protected inner waters of estuaries, laden with sediment, form the richest of all the intertidal environments of the Washington coast. Their productivity far exceeds that of either the finest agricultural land or the open ocean. The vast expanses of mudflat harbor thousands of invertebrates per cubic foot of material, which in turn, support diverse higher forms including fishes, mammals and birds. Among the "higher" forms, man is prominent. Our recognition of the value of estuaries and their fringing habitats has arrived late; much of America's original endowment of estuarine habitat has been lost to dredging and filling. Between 1958 and 1978 alone, seven percent of the nation's estuaries were destroyed. The great outer coastal estuaries of Washington—Willapa Bay and Grays Harbor—form vital links in the remaining chain of Pacific Coast estuaries.

Hardshell clams of the cobble beach, left to right: butter clam (Saxidomus giganteus); Manila *littleneck* (Tapes japonica), *and the native littleneck* (Protothaca staminea). KARNA ORSEN

The scallop (Chlamys hastata) *showing its many tiny eyes. Most scallops occur on gravelly bottoms in deeper water.* JEFF FOOTT

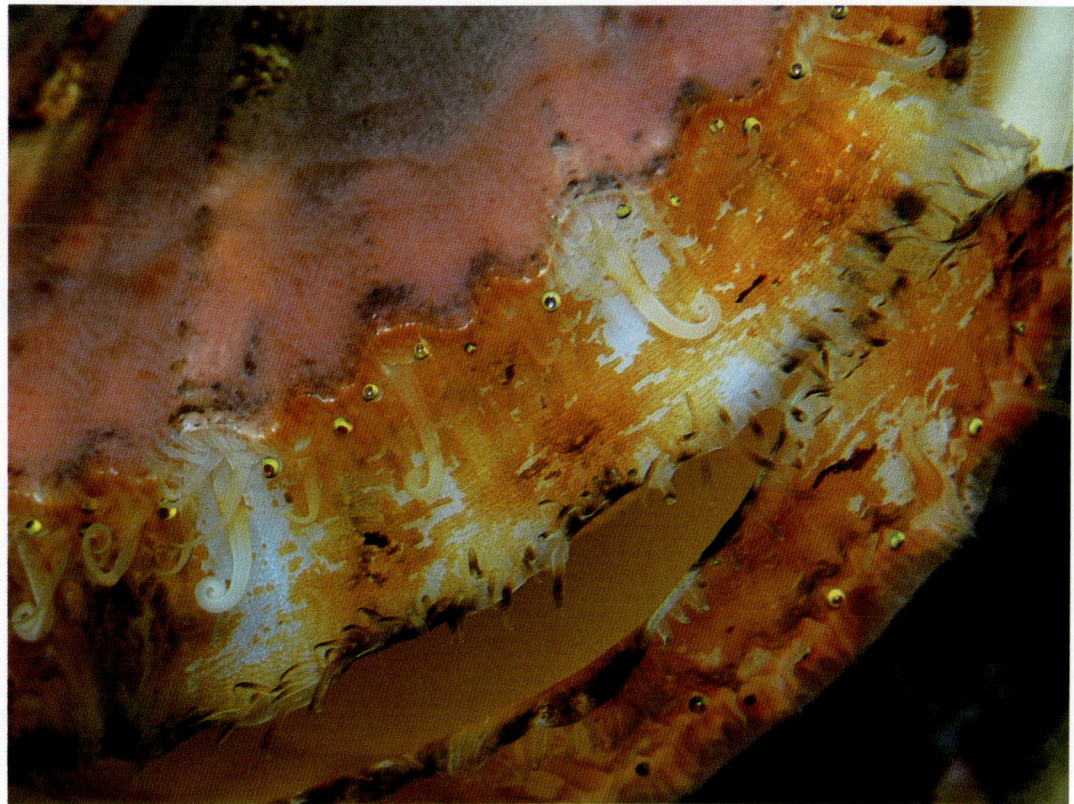

47

Coastal wetlands host a multitude of life-forms. Here, migratory shorebirds pause to feed at Bowerman Basin. Fragments of unspoiled estuaries have dwindled through decades of draining, filling and development. TOM & PAT LEESON

What makes estuaries such formidable habitats is that they serve as large traps that hold nutrients, organic debris and sediments from the terrestrial environment. Here the fresh water of rivers mixes with salt water, triggering complex chemical and physical changes. The deposition of silt in estuaries, for example, is a function not only of decreased velocity, but also of the coagulation of negatively charged clay particles by the positive ions of some metals present in sea water.

Biologically, the estuarine boundary between worlds of land and sea creates nursery environments for young salmon, feeding grounds for millions of migratory shorebirds and lush habitat for both invertebrates with no immediate "purpose" for humans and those we value the greatest. Commercial oysters in Willapa Bay alone are valued at $2 million annually, with the value of private beds set at $30 million.

An important habitat within Washington estuaries is the eelgrass bed—a lush underwater meadow that actually flowers and provides cover and sustenance for many other organisms. Eelgrass is a true flowering plant that has adapted for life in salt water. In protected shallows it blooms and produces seed that is dispersed by water currents. Eelgrass beds are complex structures, ecologically. The plant's rhizomes bind the silt and sand substrate into dense mats; its leaves undulate with the motions of water. Within its maze of passageways, green penpoint gunnels hide and roam. Bay pipefish, relatives of the seahorse, bear uncanny resemblance to the eelgrass leaves themselves. Thin stalks with fins, eyes and pursed mouths, pipefish hover erect amid the green ribbons of eelgrass foliage.

As a food source, eelgrass is the principal forage for the black brant, a diminutive sea goose that migrates along the Pacific flyway. Brant use Willapa Bay and Dungeness Bay in the Strait of Juan de Fuca as staging areas for their northward migrations to the Yukon River Delta. Tens of thousands of the birds formerly visited the regions, but the loss of critical wetlands elsewhere has cut the flocks drastically. Extensive eelgrass beds in Willapa Bay and at Dungeness were important factors in the establishment of national wildlife refuges at both sites; today skeins of brant make annual visits and feed watchfully at water's edge or safely offshore.

Conflict between human use of estuaries and that of myriad non-human life-forms is common. Around the world, the majority of humanity lives in the coastal zone. Where coastlines enclose large estuary basins, civilization and commerce thrive. Economic pressures inflate the value of wetlands and estuary margins into the realm of blue-chip industrial real estate and out of the realm of benign neglect—the state of management that usually sees them thrive best as natural environments. A poignant case study is that of Bowerman Basin, west of Hoquiam in Grays Harbor. Named for an adjacent airport, the basin sees annual visits by migratory shorebirds that number in the hundreds of thousands. During their springtime migration, western sandpipers create a winged spectacle as they mass in the intertidal zone, feeding on mud-dwelling invertebrates. In flight, they bedazzle. As if on cue, a thousand will turn as one, their countershaded bodies like a card section at a college football game flashing this color, then that. They alight, a thousand tiny beaks punching the mud for food.

The sandpipers' claim for Bowerman Basin is tenuous in the face of economic pressures to convert the habitat to other uses. Environmentalists and wildlife agencies have pressured local authorities into concessions that may see the basin preserved for shorebirds. The costs, unfortunately, are wetlands elsewhere. Development authorities, eager to get in on the ground floor of potential economic booms; to line the harbor with facilities designed to capture the wealth of the "Pacific Rim"; to bolster the gloomy economy of one of Washington's most underemployed regions, eye wistfully other parts of the Grays Harbor estuary. Bowerman can go to the sandpipers, they say, if habitat concerns will not impede the development of other sites. Lacking the hundreds of thousands of known and documented bird inhabitants, those sites, rich with living resources, will join the statistical data as estuary wetlands lost.

Rivers

One of the most powerful natural adaptations to illustrate the interrelationship between the sea and the freshwater environments is one that evolved in the fishes and is called "anadromy." Anadromy is the display of a migratory cycle punctuated by fresh- and saltwater residencies. Anadromous fishes breed in fresh water, spend varying amounts of time as juveniles there, then move to salt water to mature and fatten. It is seen most dramatically in salmonids—salmon, trout, char and smelt—but also among Washington coastal fishes in lamprey, shad and sturgeon. In members of the salmon family, the degree of anadromy displayed in a given species seems to be a reliable yardstick for determining evolutionary relationships. Some rainbow trout stocks, for example, can live out their entire lives in fresh water, while others (steelhead) make the saltwater migration. Pacific salmon, thought to have evolved from some trout-like ancestor, display obligatory anadromy in all species in their native range, although limited stocks of sockeye salmon survive without journeying to the sea in landlocked lake environments. Anadromy in salmon is thought to be an evolutionary strategy by which the species broke out of the relatively nutrient-poor ecosystems of freshwater environments and tapped the rich larder of the ocean pastures.

Such a mechanism also has brought great benefit to the terrestrial ecosystems that line rivers where salmon spawn. If the rivers are conductors of water, sediments and leeched nutrients from land to the sea, they must also be viewed as the rights-of-way of return, through which part of the ocean's lush produce is given back to the land. Anadromous fishes, particularly salmon, are the bearers.

Mist rises over a point bar on the Hoh River. Coastal rivers are explosive environments, fluctuating wildly through the seasons of flood and drought, constantly changing the physical shape of the land and the composition of living communities.
JEFF GNASS

Fishes such as salmon and steelhead that return to rivers of their birth to spawn bring with them nutrients of the sea that are recycled into the forest ecosystem.
TOM & PAT LEESON

Above: Purple and red sea urchins (Strongylocentrotus sp.). PAT O'HARA
Right: Ochre seastars (Pisaster ochraceus) *cluster around a rock—scant shelter in such a volatile environment.* KEITH D. LAZELLE

Facing page: Kelp. TIM THOMPSON

Each year thousands of fish writhe up their natal streams to lay eggs and die. The body of a salmon is a plump, self-propelled sack of fertilizer, rich in nitrates and phosphate, both of which are in short supply in the terrestrial ecosystem. Following spawning, salmon carcasses are rapidly spread through the riparian zone, distributed either by the river itself or by mammal, bird and insect scavengers. Contrary to earlier assumptions that the river system flushes most detritus downstream, where it is lost to the forest ecosystem, recent findings reveal that the bulk of carcass material is retained in the aquatic environment—in side channels, and beaver ponds—and forest floodplains, where it nourishes the forest and a host of organisms of all trophic levels.

Washington's coastal rivers are extraordinarily dynamic environments that pulse with the flood of runoff from a steep land. Biologically, they express a seasonality that witnesses complex interrelationships among schedules of various organisms. Salmon runs, for example, display timing mechanisms transmitted in the genes of the various species and populations. Limited spawning and rearing habitat are utilized by the different species at different times in an evolutionary adjustment that minimizes direct competition between species or stocks and maximizes each population's survival potential. Similarly, run timing has evolved that coincides with periods of high water to facilitate ascending the rivers; egg development occurs apace with temperature variation in the rivers, and fry emergence in some species coincides with periods of freshet that distribute the juveniles throughout the river basin, lessening competition for food during their residency.

It is extraordinarily ironic that life inhabits a coast. Such an environment is unstable to an extreme; mutable in cycles of moments, hours, tides, days, seasons, centuries and even eons. There are the violence of breaking waves, the tidal flux of submersion and exposure, the seasonal shift of shore sediments and warm-water currents, the rise and fall of the seas juggling the earth's water-budget books and the collisions and uplifts of the continents. It is a tough place to live.

But consider that, from the earliest moments of living history, the continental shore has fostered life in a spectacularly diverse array. The edges of ancient continents are memorialized in limestone and marble, in shales and sandstones, perched now among mountain aeries. From these hoary reefs and seabeds we extract the imprints and casts of exoskeletons that surrounded the soft tissues of the first animal life—only some forms of which survive today. In living communities, the complex layers of predator, prey and parasite, as well as myriad other ecological relationships, make this coastal ecosystem one of the most intricate of the temperate regions. To peer into a tidepool for the first time, seeing life in numberless and varied forms, is for most people an awakening. To comprehend, for a moment, the evolutionary significance of the act of migration in a single species gives breathless pause. The life of a coast is life at its richest.

In reconciling these contradictions, we must regard the whole. We must consider diversity itself as an effect of the coast's complex instability, rather than something that occurs in spite of it. The biological opportunity that makes the coastal zone an ecological amazement arises out of its many seeming disordering processes. Stability, if it could ever come to such a system, would result in sterility. The overall balance in this rich ecosystem is derived from the ability of living substance to mold itself into every niche of a complex and changing setting. It thrives in the dynamic tension of constant physical disruption, repeating itself in cycles— cadences that ring with the ocean's subtle pulse.

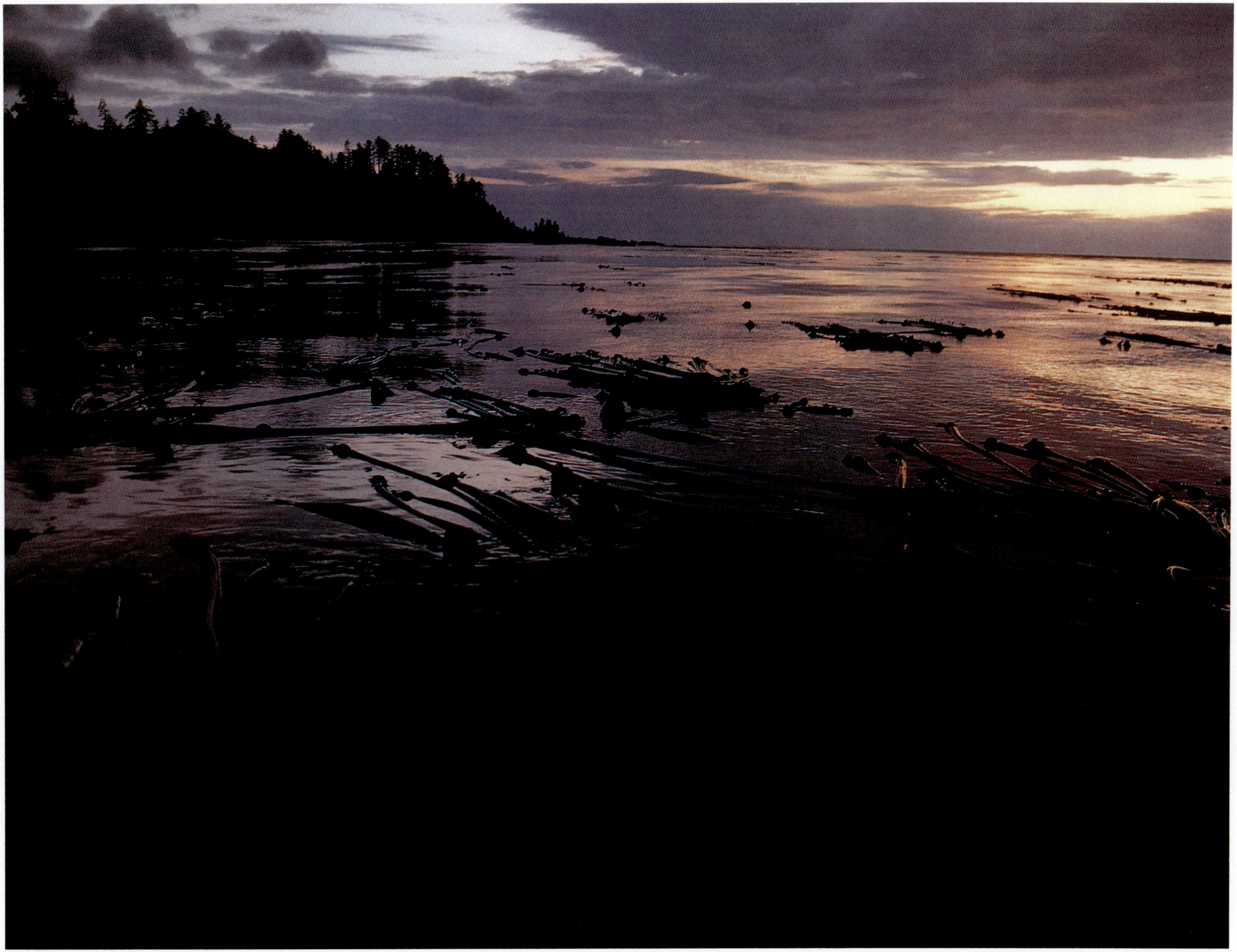

WHALES, MIGRATIONS & WHALING

The mammoth bones of the California Gray lie bleaching on the shores of those silvery waters, and are scattered along the broken coasts, from Siberia to the Gulf of California; and ere long it may be questioned whether this mammal will not be numbered among the extinct species of the Pacific.

Charles M. Scammon, 1874

Above: Makah whalers, early 1900s. ASAHEL CURTIS, COURTESY WASHINGTON STATE HISTORICAL SOCIETY

Right: Bay City Whaling Station, early 1920s. HISTORICAL PHOTO COURTESY OF JONES PHOTO CO., ABERDEEN, WA

Facing page, top: Orca whales (Orcinus orca). TIM THOMPSON.
Bottom: California gray whale. JEFF FOOTT

To Charles Scammon, a whaling captain of the late 19th century, the fate of the California gray whale seemed sadly apparent. In his lifetime, and even under his command, thousands of these migrating giants were slaughtered, and herd populations dwindled to the point that few were seen in their spring and fall migrations off the West Coast.

By 1900, these creatures were nearly extinct, and their scarcity forced commercial whalers to turn to other whale species for their catch quotas. From that time until a 17-nation treaty was ratified in 1947 to protect them, the grays just managed to survive and slowly rebuild their population strengths. Under protection, California grays have recovered in number to what some consider to be near-original population levels.

The life-history of the gray whale is punctuated by seasonal migrations that, in distance, exceed those of any other mammal. These semi-annual journeys take them from Baja California to the Bering and Chukchi Seas and back down the Pacific Coast—a round trip of 20,000 miles. As bottom foragers, grays feed in shallow water where they can "root" large quantities of mud- and sand-dwelling molluscs and amphipods. Only the broad continental shelf regions of the Bering and Chukchi Seas support populations of these organisms in quantities sufficient, in turn, to support the grays. Here, the whales build up fat reserves that will fuel their migration south and sustain them through the winter. Forced south by sea ice, the grays move to the warm, protected nearshore waters of Mexico, where they expend less energy on metabolic activity. In the Mexican lagoons, the calves are born and rapidly gain size and strength needed for the northward journey. During both legs of the journey, most of the whales travel close to shore, moving day and night at a speed of about five miles per hour.

For countless generations, migrating grays were preyed upon by the Makah people from their ancestral redoubt at Cape Flattery. The slow movement of the pods, or whale herds, past the cape signalled an important period of food gathering for the tribe, as well as a time when the strongest and bravest hunters met their severest test. The hunt was highly formalized—select cadres of whalers ventured offshore in large canoes, risking their lives as they stalked their quarry among the heaving swells.

Grays were hunted in historic times by American whalers who discovered that during the winter months the grays congregated in Baja's lagoons and, in spite of their inferior baleen (whalebone) and smaller quantities of oil, were easily cornered and killed. It therefore made little sense to voyage to the far north in search of bowhead and right whales, or wander the seas looking for sperm whales. Lagoon whaling decimated the populations, shifting the hunt to other species and, eventually, to other methods of whaling.

Although California gray whale populations dwindled to levels that precluded their harvest, whaling for other species, primarily humpback, fin and sperm whales, was conducted off the Washington Coast between 1911 and 1925. Killer boats stationed at Bay City on Grays Harbor ranged off the coast, killing whales as far south as Cape Blanco, Oregon, and north to Vancouver Island. Most kills were made within a 135-mile radius of the whaling station. Carcasses were towed to Bay City, where they were processed—annual production of oil averaged 5,400 barrels. Decreasing demand for whale oil and declining numbers of the quarry, brought the operation to a halt in 1925. In 1935, the whaling station burned.

Today, whales again visit the Washington Coast without the threat of slaughter. Grays make their semi-annual passages, traveling south between October and December; moving north between February and May. The best months for observation are March through May. Excellent shore viewing is afforded at Cape Flattery, Cape Alava, various bluff overlooks near Kalaloch, Point Grenville and Cape Disappointment. Charter boats conduct offshore trips from Ilwaco, Westport, Neah Bay and Sekiu. Orca and Minke whales are commonly seen during summer months in the Strait of Juan de Fuca and around the San Juan Islands. Minkes congregate near Cattle Point, at the southern tip of San Juan Island and Orcas range throughout the islands but are commonly seen near Lime Kiln Lighthouse, on San Juan Island's western shore. Numerous cruise operators schedule whale-watch trips in and around the San Juans.

CHAPTER FOUR

STRAIT OF JUAN DE FUCA

Black oystercatcher. JEFF FOOTT

Right: Sunrise. Dungeness light twinkles as daylight grows. Smith Island rests in the shade of Mt. Baker. PAT O'HARA

They're coming in now, winged bricks that travel 30 miles an hour, just two feet above the crimson water. Rhinoceros auklets are returning to Protection Island in the fiery twilight, gathering in the near-shore shadows, before they return to their burrows on the island's bluffs. Some are inbound from the west; those that spend their days upsound arrive from the east. Nearly 34,000 rhinoceros auklets—50 percent of all breeding rhinos in the lower 48 states—are converging here tonight, as on every other night through the summer weeks of the breeding season. Above us on the bluffs, pelagic cormorants are perched on thin ledges of the gravel cliff, squatting erect on seaweed nests. Their forms are dark and graceful, like chador-wrapped women atop ancient city walls. Sounds—wails, shrieks and avian gossip—fill the air like the verbal commerce of hawking vendors. This egg bazaar is the largest pelagic cormorant nesting colony in Washington. In the gathering dusk the familiar outline of the Olympic Mountains and the passing light blip of Dungeness lighthouse are the only reference points that place me on the Strait of Juan de Fuca and not in some bird-world equivalent of the Middle East.

The Strait is both a familiar setting and one exotic. It owes its familiarity to a fundamental perspective that many Washingtonians share. We commonly look across water—Puget Sound, Rosario Strait, Hood Canal and so on. We see water horizons broken by distant heights and other land. Like these, the Strait of Juan de Fuca is easily absorbed in the scenery of the day-to-day. But its exotic qualities, its moments and places seemingly disconnected from other mundane experience, can be startling. As a world unto itself, the Strait is all but unknown. In the waning light, seeing these birds confirms my hunch that even though the Strait of Juan de Fuca's presence is obvious, its inner workings remain unseen.

It is to Captain Cook that the precedent can be traced. If the Great Navigator's ghost lingers over worlds that he charted, the error he committed with respect to the Strait of Juan de Fuca must rankle him no end. Upon reaching the latitude of "the pretended Strait of Juan de Fuca" in 1778, Cook gloated, "we saw nothing like it, nor is there the least probability that iver any such thing exhisted [*sic*]."

Cook's oversight is commonly explained away by a lingering fog bank and threatening squall. The Captain's Britannic pride might as easily have prompted the ill-made remark, for it came at a time when empires were being made and lost by proving or disproving loose accounts of continental shores and strategic passages to the Orient. Cook, a subject of the King of England, also claimed fidelity to an exploratory style that placed cartographic precision above hearsay, especially that of a Greek pilot working under a pseudonym for a rival nation and dead for centuries. Before Cook's eyes was the Strait. Unbelieving, he failed to see.

Rumors of the fabled strait had been bandied about ever since 1592, when a Greek pilot, Apostolos Valerianos (a.k.a. Juan de Fuca), reported that he had located the Strait of Anian after cruising north from Acapulco, then naval headquarters of the Spanish on North America's west coast. In his story, Juan de Fuca entered the strait, traveled for 20 days, reached the Atlantic, and returned to Acapulco. The story was popularized by cartographer Guillaume Delisle and teetered between the worlds of truth and fiction for nearly 200 years before a strait was actually discovered that might, or might not, have been the one the old Greek saw or dreamed.

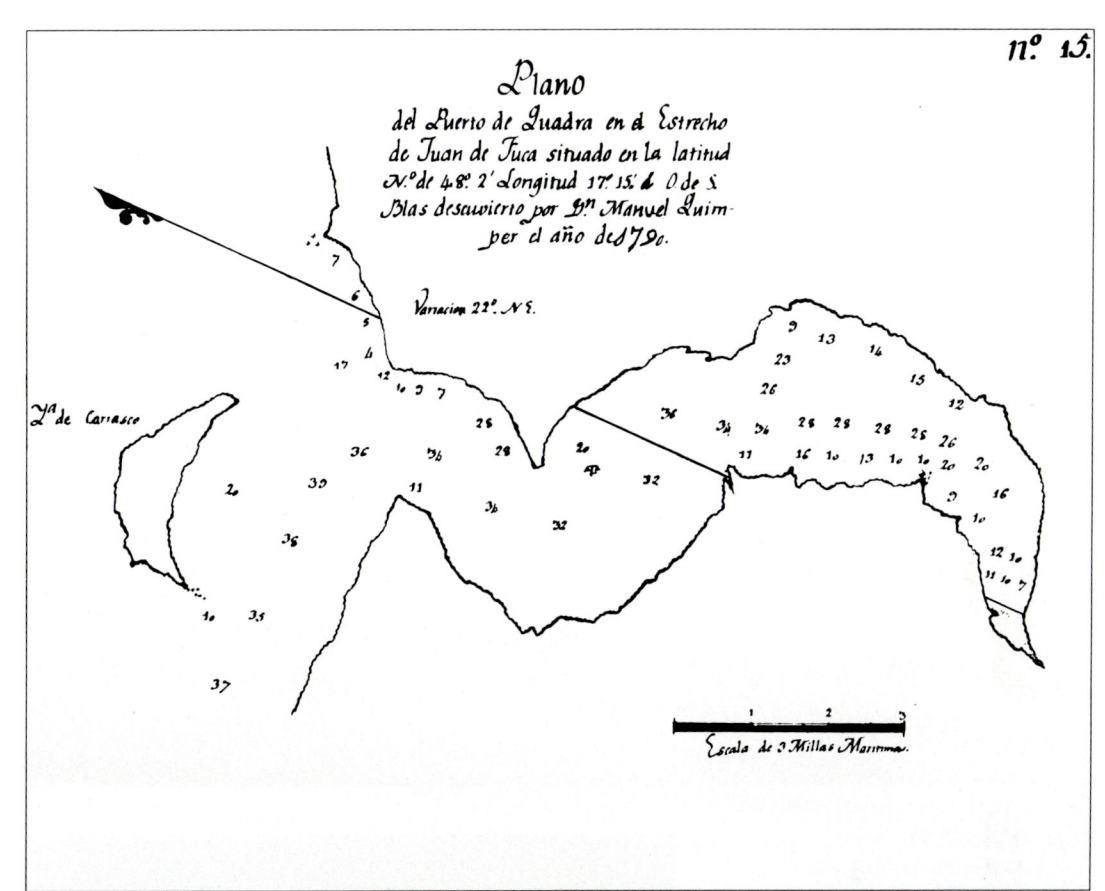

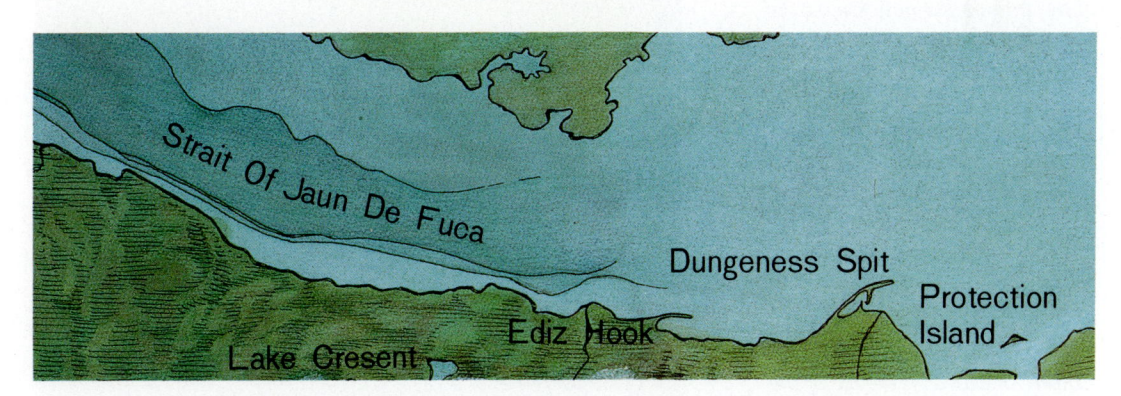

Top: Known to the Spanish before Vancouver, Carrasco's Isle and Puerto de Quadra now bear English names—Protection Island and Discovery Bay. COURTESY MINISTERIO ASUNTOS EXTERIORES AND MUSEO NAVAL, MADRID

Point Wilson light, established in 1879, marks the entrance to Admiralty Inlet—the northern arm of the inland sea now known as Puget Sound. FRANK S. BALTHIS

Salmon and halibut attract sport fishers from afar to the resource-rich waters of the Strait. TIM THOMPSON

Facing page: Scant rain makes the Dungeness Valley one of the driest coastal areas north of San Diego County. Located in the lee of the Olympic Mountains, "rainshadow" farmland must be irrigated.
PAT O'HARA

The Strait's discovery has been popularly attributed to Captain Charles William Barkley, who visited the region in 1787. This account too remains fuzzy, for although the diary entry of Barkley's bride is very clear, its authenticity is not. It seems that Mrs. Barkley's original diary was lost in a fire—the account we have today is the recollection of Captain John T. Walbran, the only person who claims to have read the original document before it perished.

Bona fide accounts of early visits to de Fuca's Strait begin with the Spanish. Shuttling between Pacific ports of Mexico and Nootka Sound, on the Pacific shore of northern Vancouver Island, Spanish ships maintained a regional presence to bolster their claim to the coastal territory. In June of 1789, Don Jose Maria Narvaez made a brief junket from Nootka to the vicinity of the entrance to the Strait of Juan de Fuca, appraised its breadth and returned to Nootka with a report of the discovery.

His commanding officer, Don Esteban Jose Martinez, who had a hunch that the Strait really did exist, was quite pleased. In his own report, Martinez concluded that the Strait must surely communicate with the Mississippi River. Martinez' veracity is dubious in retrospect, not just for his outsized claim for the Strait, but also for the fact that he nearly started a war between England and Spain by capturing several English vessels and imprisoning their crews, a move embarrassing to Spain. His actions made Nootka, and the Northwest, the fulcrum of Spain and England's growing global seesaw in their bitter struggle for world sea dominance.

Subsequent visits to the Strait by Spaniards Eliza and Quimper, American Robert Gray and Englishman George Vancouver failed to reveal more than the fact that it penetrates North America fewer than a hundred miles. Instead of being an authoritative rent in the continental fabric, the Strait of Juan de Fuca ends a short distance inland, and branches into narrow inland seas that extend in both northerly and southerly directions.

Although the Strait failed the hopes of world navigators bent on a strategic shortcut to the Orient, its worldly importance today is very real. It separates two large nations and forms a link that connects each to the economies of many others, especially along the Pacific Rim. Included among favored-trade nations is the emergent China, a modern equivalent of far-off Cathay, hungering for Western goods now as when it hungered for sea otter pelts.

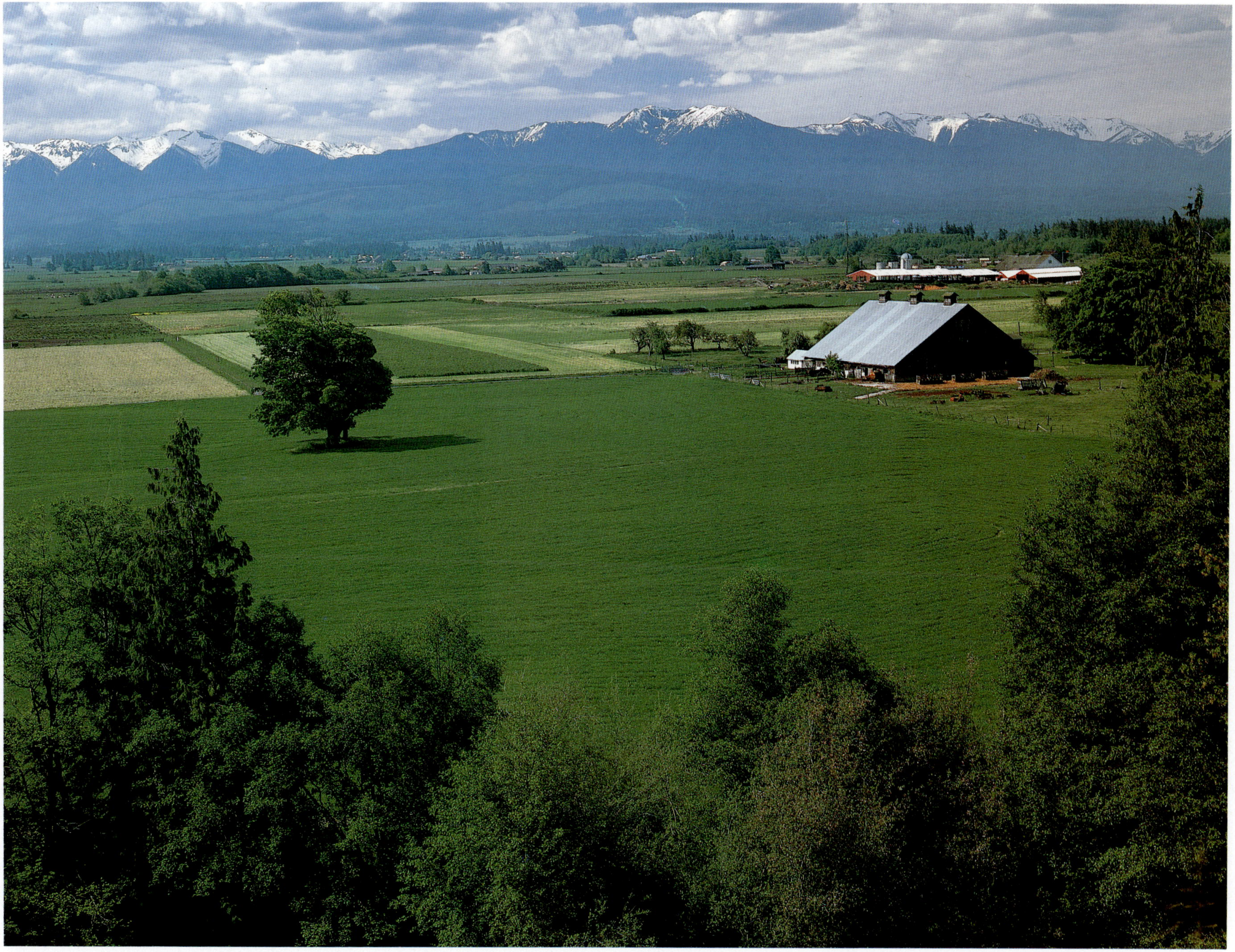

Vancouver Island, cut from geologic fabric different from that of the Olympic Peninsula, looms beyond the Strait. CINDY McINTYRE

Facing page, left: Brittle cactus (Opuntia fragilis) *surprised early naturalists and settlers who found it on the dry prairies that line the eastern strait. Few plants remain on the Olympic Peninsula—fewer yet flower at this outpost of the plant's native range.* ROBERT STEELQUIST
Right: Hopes of a railroad terminus ran high in Port Townsend—hopes unfulfilled. That optimism, however, left its legacy. The Hastings House was built in 1889. PAT O'HARA

Through this crowded sea lane pass about 1,000 cargo-laden vessels each month, carrying Pacific Northwest products out and the world's products in and serving the busy ports of Vancouver, B.C., Seattle and Tacoma. On a clear day an end-view of the crowded traffic lanes can foreshorten the distance, compressing a line of ships spread over 20 miles into what seems like a ticket line at a movie house. Hyundai automobiles, Prudhoe Bay crude oil, western hemlock logs and thousands of other products of the world at large transit the Strait, balancing the excesses of some nations with the needs of others. A modern form of 18th-century world dominance hangs in the balance—trade and economic growth.

Yet the Strait is not always a serene host. Its history is punctuated with catastrophes. More than 200 ships have been lost at its entrance, giving rise to its nickname, "Graveyard of the Pacific." Despite electronic navigational aids, vessel traffic control systems and ships that power themselves against wind and current, pilots must reckon constantly with the Strait's surging flood, ebb, fog and other traffic. The odds alone dictate that maritime disaster can strike through human frailty, as it did on December 21, 1985, when the ARCO *Anchorage*, on a routine stopover in Port Angeles harbor, grounded and spilled an estimated 240,000 gallons of Alaskan crude oil. A pilot's error was cited as the cause of the spill, the worst in Puget Sound history. Experts placed the mortality among seabirds, mostly grebes and diving ducks, at near 4,000. One week after the spill, partially emulsified oil formed a string-like slick along the Olympic Peninsula shore from Dungeness Spit to Cape Flattery. While the short-term impact appears to have been light, long-term effects continue to be studied.

The Strait of Juan de Fuca can be viewed from other perspectives as well. Geologically, it is a prominent boundary in the earth's crust, where the remains of a tropical island subcontinent that make up much of the parent rock of Vancouver Island meet the deformed mass of ocean crust that forms the Olympic Peninsula. Recent geological investigations reveal that Vancouver Island is part of a well traveled "terrane" known as Wrangellia. Wrangellia was once a Japan-sized island subcontinent carried on the moving crust of the ocean floor from equatorial latitudes. Its collision with North America, sometime between 200 and 140 million years ago, left it smeared across today's continent from Southeast Alaska to Hells Canyon, Idaho. The Queen Charlotte Islands and Vancouver Island represent some of the wreckage.

The Olympic Peninsula is the result of a more recent continent-building episode. Volcanic material spread over the abyssal sediments as an underwater volcano chain spewed molten basalt from submarine fissures between 55 and 30 million years ago. Carried together by movement of the Juan de Fuca Plate, these interleaved volcanic and sedimentary rocks collided with the continental edge between 30 and 12 million years ago. The Olympic Mountains, a horseshoe of basalt volcanics mingled with sandstones and shales of the ancient seafloor, form a distinct addition to the continental margin—the latest in a series of jarring collisions that have added nearly all of what is now Washington State to North America.

The Strait of Juan de Fuca that we know today received its rough form during the last Ice Age, when glaciers swept south from the Canadian coast ranges into lowland areas of western Washington. One vast ice sheet split into two lobes around the upthrust Olympics, the Puget Lobe gouging the depression now filled with Puget Sound, the Juan de Fuca Lobe carving the Strait. It is estimated that the thickness of the ice exceeded 3,000 feet. The seaward-bound lobe gradually thinned into an ice shelf in the vicinity of the present entrance to the Strait, calving great bergs that drifted away on the chilly Pacific of 10,000 years ago.

Additional finishing work continues as the soft deposits of glacier-laid gravel erode under the relentless force of wave action. Pale bluffs line both shores of the Strait in many places, composed of clay, silt, sand and gravel that was compacted by the weight of the glacier. As this loose material is undercut by wave action, it collapses. Near-shore currents run brown with sediments as the finer debris is carried along the shore to be deposited on some nearby sand spit. Both Ediz Hook, the gentle arm that encloses Port Angeles Harbor, and Dungeness Spit, reported to be the longest natural sand spit on earth, owe their existence to soft bluffs and the prevailing wave patterns that are unique to the Strait.

The Strait forms a tongue of ocean that penetrates a region of dense forests, carrying with it life-forms of the

Harbor seals (Phoca vitulina) *are the most abundant marine mammals of the Strait.* JEFF FOOTT

Seal Rock, western Strait of Juan de Fuca. ROBERT STEELQUIST

pelagic world—storm petrels and minke whales—into the midst of a terrestrial world of coyotes and conifers. As a biological resource it is a marine wilderness of unlikely encounters and exotic visitations. Millions of salmon course along its reefs and through its kelp beds, compelled toward spawning beds in hundreds of rivers. Orca whales of "L-pod," a group of between 40 and 50 animals with customary haunts off the west coast of Vancouver Island, follow the inbound salmon through the Strait and into the labyrinth of passages among the San Juan Islands.

Gray whales migrating between the birthing lagoons of Baja California and the feeding waters of the Bering occasionally nose into the Strait. One immature male observed near Port Angeles in December 1985 apparently stayed through the winter instead of making the southward trip to Mexico.

Elephant seals, the largest pinnipeds of the northern hemisphere, make rare appearances in the Strait. In 1977 a female was seen in Discovery Bay. Its tag revealed it to be a member of the breeding population located on Ano Nuevo Island, south of San Francisco. The more common harbor seals breed in large groups at a variety of locations along the Strait. Most significant among these sites are Minor Island, Protection Island, Dungeness Spit and Race Rocks.

The shores of the Strait host migratory waterfowl pausing from journeys that stretch from Mexico to Alaska. Black brant, a diminutive sea goose that breeds in Alaska, gathers into large flocks, feeding in the shallows that line the Strait. A recently discovered hawk migration route crosses the Strait's entrance—hundreds of raptors each day pass above the rocky headlands at Cape Flattery during the migration's peak.

Sea life thrives here in a multitude of forms: soft-bodied cup corals; iridescent sluglike nudibranchs; the silvery monster of the deep, the king salmon; Pacific octopus (the world's largest species). Giant halibut hug the bottom as they roam "game trails" in search of octopus and other prey. Crowds of sea urchins swarm over the rocky bottom, grazing on algae. So rich are the urchin stocks that a commercial fishery is well established for these spiny relatives of starfish and sand dollars.

Marine habitats found in the Strait are diverse, from sandy bottoms that support submerged meadows of eelgrass to rainforest-like kelp beds, where sunlight filters through a lush canopy of undulating fronds. The rocky intertidal zone reveals fierce competition for space and a host of strategies for survival in an environment sometimes beneath, sometimes above, water. Reefs, banks, shoals, mud flats, submarine canyons and cliffs form a topography that would jar our sensibilities if we could see it. We know it only as a lead-colored plain, a liquid prairie with a steady, smooth horizon.

De Fuca's Strait is a critical link, in every sense, in the history, economy, culture and natural environment of the coastal region of Washington and British Columbia. Yet, it is largely overlooked against the backdrop of opportunity of the land itself and the world beyond. It remains unbridged and undammed, and not unlike on Cook's day of pride, unnoticed.

For the watchful, however, the Strait presents itself in many ways. Those who live and work with it know it as wild and alive. It is an area of scenic beauty on a grand scale. Its shores are mostly unpeopled, allowing glimpses of an earlier Northwest from vistas like Shark's Reef on Lopez Island, Protection Island, or Slip Point, near Clallam Bay.

Where civilization marks the shore, it is dwarfed so much by the enormity of the Strait itself that cities are lost in the distance—marked only by the steam plumes of paper mills, the twinkle of night lights, the smudge of exhaust fumes. Thus outscaled, cities and towns lose their grip as dominating land forms, yielding to spectacular mountain backdrops and foregrounds of water.

The Strait of Apostolos Valerianos—Juan de Fuca, if you prefer—does exist at 48 degrees, 30 minutes, North Latitude. Cook's lacuna, in retrospect, was unfortunate. Yet even though its presence is now unquestioned, the Strait remains embedded in the blind spot that many have for the close-at-hand.

Left: Snowy owl (Nyctea scandiaca)—*winter visitor at Dungeness National Wildlife Refuge.* KEITH D. LAZELLE

Above: Dungeness Spit. ROSS HAMILTON

PROTECTION ISLAND

Protection Island National Wildlife Refuge. PAT O'HARA

At five a.m. on July 11, 1790, Sub-Lieutenant Manuel Quimper ordered a longboat over the side of the sloop, *Princesa Real,* to be commanded by his second pilot Juan Carrasco. The pilot and his crew were to row southeast from the ship, anchored off the mouth of the Dungeness River, and examine a point of land visible in the distance. Twelve hours later, the boat returned and reported a good harbor, its entrance guarded by an island. Quimper named the island Isla de Carrasco—Carrasco's Isle. The port he named Quadra, after the commandante at the Spanish naval base at San Blas. The port was described as ample—able to "hold many vessels by reason of its size and shelter."

Just less than two years later, Isla de Carrasco received its present name from Capt. Vancouver. Unaware that the Strait had been navigated previously by the Spanish, he applied English names to coastal features that he added to his charts. His "discovery" of Carrasco's Isle took place on May 1, 1792, when, under circumstances similar to Quimper's, he anchored his ships near the Dungeness River and explored eastward by longboat. Later describing his ramble on the island with Vancouver, the naturalist Menzies wrote: "On ascending the Bank to the summit of the Island, a rich lawn beautified with nature's luxuriant bounties burst at once on our view & impressed us with no less pleasure than novelty—It was abundantly cropped with a variety of grass clover & wild flowers, here & there adornd by aged pines with wide spreading boughs & well shelterd by a slip of them densely copsed with Underwood stretching along the summit of the steep sandy cliff, the whole seeming if it had been laid out from the premeditated plan of a judicious designer."

Vancouver too noted the island's park-like appearance in his journal but was more taken by the harbor which opened to the south, and the mountain landscape that arose beyond and to the west. The island he named "Protection"; the harbor, "Port Discovery," after his ship. Availing himself of the fine harbor, Vancouver anchored there nearly three weeks, conducting astronomical observations, "airing" the powder, further exploring the waterways to the southeast (including the entrance to Puget Sound), allowing the crews some much-needed relaxation ashore, and enabling Menzies the opportunity to search for new species of plants and animals on and around Protection Island.

The Scottish naturalist was well rewarded for his efforts. The forests and coastal bluffs surrounding Port Discovery were ablaze with wildflowers. In their initial approach to the island, Menzies noted "vast flights of water fowl such as Auks Divers Ducks & Wild Geese." Elsewhere in the vicinity, he collected fishes using a beach seine and he caught a small animal with an offensive smell that he concluded (too late) to be a skunk. Pacific madrone, Pacific rhododendron and hairy manzanita were all described for science for the first time from his collections there. On his last visit ashore on Protection, Menzies discovered an inconspicuous cactus, the fragile prickly pear, which surprised him in its northerly occurrence. Although Menzies' journals were not published for many decades, Protection Island was noted by its first naturalist observer to be fertile habitat—ripe with "nature's luxuriant bounties."

Detailed knowledge of Protection Island's bird colonies came in 1859, with the publication of the railroad survey reports created under the direction of Washington's territorial governor, Isaac Stevens. Dr. George Suckley, an army surgeon as well as one of the survey expedition naturalists, referred to rhinoceros auklets when he called Protection Island "a favorite breeding ground of the species where they breed in holes dug in the steep banks." Ironically, at about the same time the first settlement of Protection Island took place—and the conflict between the island as habitat for people and the island as habitat for seabirds arose.

In 1859, James G. Swan reported a visit to the homesteads of gentlemen by the names of Shane and Buffington, who took up claims on the island with the intention of farming. The light prairie soil admitted the plow readily and bountiful crops of oats and potatoes were grown. Shane and Buffington apparently did not stay long. Over the years and dozens of landowners, however, the island was less fruitful for crops than for forage. Cattle and sheep became the dominant lifeforms, chewing the once-luxuriant cover to stubble and pounding a tracery of paths on

Cobble and drift. PAT O'HARA

Paintings by Zella Schultz, left to right:
Rhinoceros auklet (Cerorhinca monocerata).
Tufted puffin (Lunda cirrhata).
Pigeon guillemot (Cepphus columba).
Black oystercatcher (Haematopus bachmani).

the island's slopes. In 100 years of occupation, parts of the island landscape were reduced to sand dunes and blowouts. On two occasions fire swept over the entire island, destroying beach logs, prairie cover and the fringes of windblown forest that line part of the upland. In addition to the physical alteration, the island's natural communities were changed by the addition of exotic species. Several varieties of pheasant were introduced—one study of pheasant documented a classic exponential growth curve followed by a dramatic crash. In addition, alfalfa was sown to cover overgrazed and wind-eroded sites on the island. Delicate mechanisms that ordered the island's natural populations of plants and animals had been upset catastrophically.

Protection's era of pastoral abuse ended in the 1960s when real estate developers began the second phase of exploitation of the island. The isolation of the island had dramatic appeal to prospective retirees and recreation-home buyers. By now too, seabird biologists were being drawn to Protection to study the rhinoceros auklets and other seabirds known to nest there. A pioneering study conducted through the mid-1950s by Frank Richardson shed new light on the night-breeding habits of the island's auklets and Protection's tenuous ecological balance. Nevertheless, little could be done to halt what seemed like an endless string of speculative ventures that all threatened the seabird habitat—it was painfully obvious to many that further study would serve only to document the island's loss as wildlife habitat.

Another seabird biologist with intense interest in Protection Island was Zella Schultz, who spent many years banding glaucous-winged gulls on the island. Schultz, who had studied bird plumage as a graduate student, also began making paintings of the seabirds found at Protection and elsewhere. An active member of the Seattle Audubon Society, she enlisted support among regional birders for a refuge long before there was a glimmer of hope that it could ever come about. By 1968, developers' ambitions for Protection reached their apogee. On this isolated fragment of upland prairie, located one and a half miles from the Olympic Peninsula mainland, they proposed a tract development that would divide the island's 394 acres into more than 1,000 90- by 100-foot lots and would house somewhere between 2,000 and 4,000 people—particularly during the summer months, when the aukery was running full tilt. What cattle and sheep could not kill, island residents, their household pets and pests surely would.

The plan fell under its own weight because of a natural limiting factor that has governed the island for hundreds (perhaps thousands) of years—the absence of water.

While speculators and their planners minimized the scope of the problem, hundreds of lots were sold, a salt marsh dredged to form a marina, roads bulldozed, underground water lines laid and an airstrip cleared. On several occasions, state health department officials found that potable water barged from the mainland had been extended with brackish water from the island's condemned wells. In 1974, the conservation community won its first victory—county officials imposed a total ban on building permits, forcing the plan to a halt. Nevertheless, buyers continued to invest in property, urged on by developers who promised a forthcoming solution.

Conservationists, gaining momentum in their effort to save as much of the island as possible, won another victory in 1974. That year the Nature Conservancy purchased 48 acres of land that contained part of the critical auklet habitat and arranged for its transfer to the Washington Department of Game, for use as a wildlife sanctuary. Zella Schultz died the same month the purchase was made and she was memorialized in its naming—the Zella M. Schultz Seabird Sanctuary.

In spite of the beachhead established with the creation of a refuge on the western end of the island, nesting populations of auklets, black oystercatchers, pelagic cormorants, pigeon guillemots and glaucous-winged gulls and a sizeable herd of harbor seals on other parts of the island remained imperiled. One development company after another assumed control, then faded into corporate oblivion. A few residences took shape, their owners increasingly embittered at both the mysterious nature of the developers' dealings and the growing conservationist hue and cry to wrest the remainder of the island out of private ownership and into the hands of the U.S. Fish and Wildlife Service.

At the heart of the environmental consort was Eleanor Stopps, an Auduboner from nearby Port Ludlow, who had been introduced to the island and its birds by Zella Schultz. Stopps patiently marshalled her facts, built a national awareness of the resource and its risk of loss, assembled a powerful alliance of environmental organizations and scientists, and educated Washington's congressional delegation on the need for national wildlife refuge status for the beleaguered isle.

In 1982, she won. On October 15, 192 years after the arrival of the Spanish pilot, President Ronald Reagan signed the legislation that created Protection Island National Wildlife Refuge. For Carrasco's Isle, for the "grass clover & wild flowers" of Menzies, for thousands of rhinoceros auklets and other seabirds, and for the legacy of Zella Schultz and for Eleanor Stopps, her protegee, Protection had arrived.

PAINTINGS COURTESY OF LUCILLE MUNZ, FROM THE JOHN W. THOMPSON COLLECTION, MARYSVILLE, WA

CHAPTER FIVE
THE NORTH COAST

PAT O'HARA

Right: Second Beach, Olympia National Park. WOLFGANG KAEHLER

Facing page: Ruby Beach, Olympic National Park. PAT O'HARA

The fog is dissipating. The coast has been locked in somber monochrome through much of the day and now the wisps are separating. Glare—noise for the eye—pours off the choppy surface of the water. Because of the sun's low angle, the thin veil of diffusing mist breaks the light into shards that seem to skitter over the waves. It's hard to look into late afternoon sky without squinting. The harsh rays of light seem to be coming from everywhere. They bounce amid the crosscurrents of converging ripples, glisten off scattered tidepools, glazing the bare, wet rocks. Even the clouds have a gloss. The slanted light pours into the cove like surging water, contained in the tiny cusp between the headlands. With darkness will come its ebb.

Even now, while the sky opens, the land is darkening. Relief from the pins of light comes by focusing on the dark islands, backlit and dim. High on the shoulders of the offshore rocks, tufts of grass comb the light, glowing in soft yellows and greens. Flagged trees are blackened silhouettes. The shadow of the island rests, spread on the incoming water as the advancing bore crosses the foreground toward me. The forest behind me spills darkness from beneath the canopy of Sitka spruce, frosted blue-green. Ochres and tans warm the rocks, and the stems of ubiquitous salmonberry show dull brown through the sparse remnants of their yellowed, decaying leaves. The light is changing, flowing out of the day. The tide is flowing in.

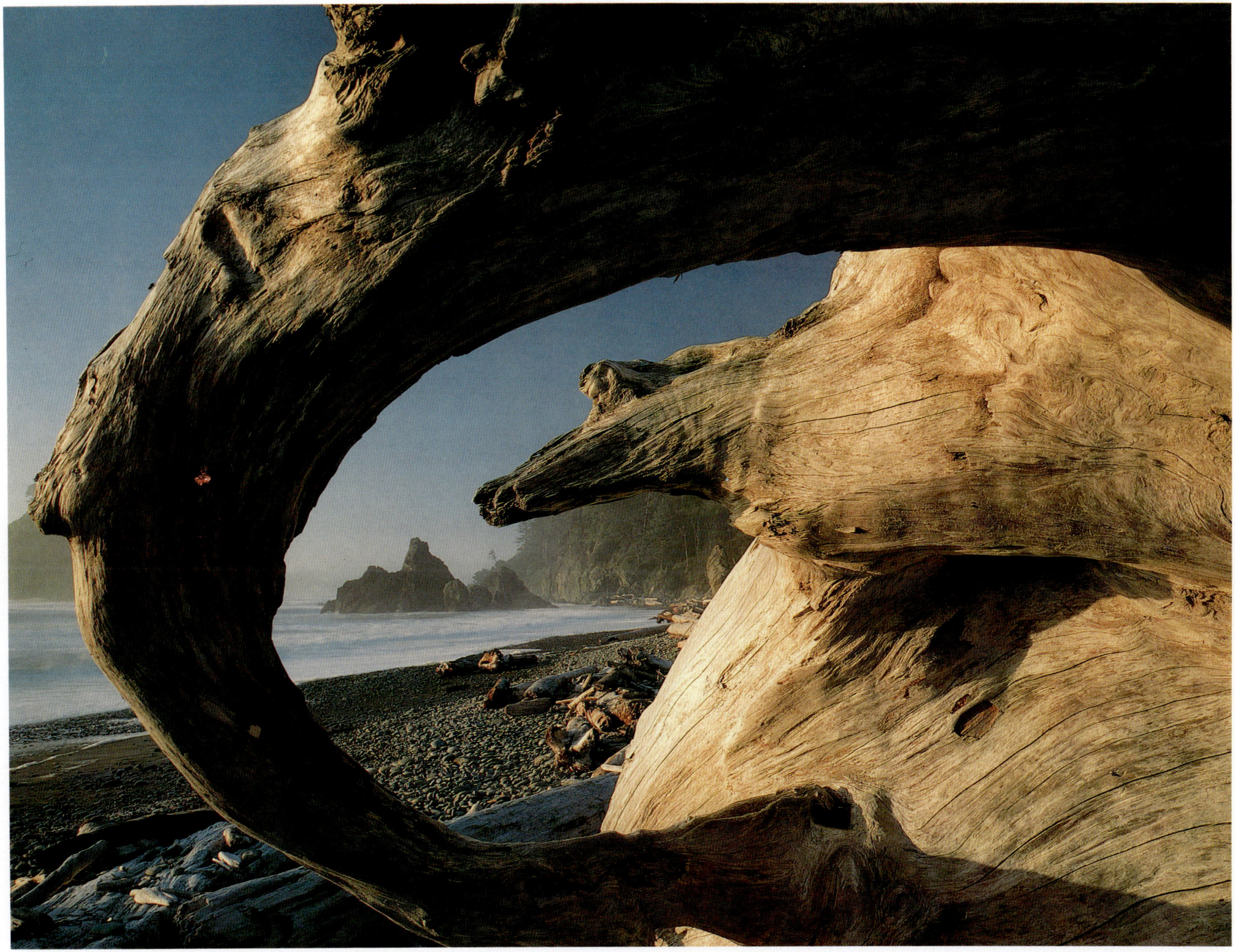

Washington's North Coast is its wild coast—broken in its contour and blunt in its appearance. The interface of land and sea is a series of tight coves, sweeping cobble and coarse-sand beaches, and broken headlands—points tipped with bare rock pinnacles. Here, the steepened land crowds the water; rolling forms of forested hillsides break sharply into angled cliff-faces, with surging breakers at their feet. Drift-strewn beaches and yellow clay banks mark the edge of the the Olympics, the edge of Washington, and the edge of the visible continent.

Little room has ever existed between the breakers and the dense forests in which people could settle and prosper. Native coastal peoples found what habitable footholds the coast presents and occupy these places today—the villages of La Push, Hoh, Queets and Taholah. The settler's urge went requited for the few who could stand the isolation, but even that hold slackened because of the acid soil, the merciless weather and the sheer distance from the rest of humanity.

Today's northern coast in Washington remains virtually uninhabited, much the same in appearance as when Spain's sailors of the cross, England's sailors of the chronometer and early fur merchants—sailors of commerce—appeared on the horizon and maintained respectful distance from the coast's forbidding visage. Parts of the coast remain the only wild coast in the lower 48 states, preserved in Olympic National Park. Other parts remain largely uninhabited because they offer little comfort and no particular advantage.Only where broad rivers meet the salt water are there navigable harbors, and the majority of those admit only skiffs and small vessels.

Conditions of wildness favor lifeforms other than human. Nesting colonies of murres, storm-petrels, auklets, puffins and cormorants crowd cliffs and bluff faces on the unreachable islets. Harbor seals and sea lions haul themselves out onto rock nubbins that stud the shore. Peregrine falcons and bald eagles soar the forest edge and rear their nestlings in the secrecy of the forbidding spruce-tops. Broad shelves of the intertidal zone alternate between exposure and concealment of tidal flux, nurturing rich communities of fishes and invertebrates—colorful meadows of animal life that compete for space, food and shelter on the wave-swept scour platforms of eroding rock. And into this wilderness, people advance only temporarily—a crab boat setting its pots, a troller dragging its bright lures, hikers in colorful rain gear traversing the cobble beach.

Efforts to conserve ecosystems of the wild coast actually began early in the 20th century, with the 1907 executive order of President Theodore Roosevelt that created the Flattery Rocks, Quillayute Needles and Copalis Rock National Wildlife Refuges. The order set aside a long and uneven string of approximately 130 islets and seabound rocks for the preservation of nesting habitat for seabirds.

Biological investigation of the offshore rocks was undertaken in 1906 by William L. Dawson, who traveled by "staunch cedar canoe" from Point Grenville to Neah Bay with his wife and young son, exploring each major rock en route and enumerating its feathered inhabitants. Dawson's accounts appeared in both the technical ornithological literature and popular magazines, and shed light for the first time on the rocky coast as a whole. In his accounts, Dawson chose a name for the Olympics' outer rank of pinnacles: "Because of their proximity, considered as a whole, to the Olympic Mountains, and because they are in a sense a by-product of the same orogenetic movement, I have proposed for these western islands the name Olympiades (pronounced Olympiah'-deez)." Although the name failed to stick, it evokes today a particular romance as though these rock spires and islands, as unapproachable to most people as the stars themselves, form some close but aloof constellation.

Dawson's family excursion was anything but easy. With two able Indian boatmen handling the canoe, the party plunged happily through the swells, and Dawson was able to inspect cliff faces and offshore rocks to his ornithological satisfaction, collecting bird eggs and making photographs. Evening, however, brought with it the necessity to land, crossing the no-man's-land of deadly surf. Between Cape Elizabeth and Destruction Island, the fog closed in:

"We had no compass, and so dared not lose track of the sound of the surf. The grayness was appalling and the sea yawned all the more limitless that we could not see it. The senior boatman, hardened veteran, but thinking most of the mother and child, said, 'Nika hiu kwass.' (I am very much afraid.)… Our salvation lay in 'Destruction,' and its earnest [sic] was to be the melancholy blast of the foghorn….Time came at last when we had to abandon the ominous assurance of the breakers and to trust to the voice alone. Out across the darkened waters we crept, following the resonant gleam. Oh, how sweet that pensive voice became!…Once, twice, three times the blast

Above: Contorted headlands near Cape Flattery. TIM THOMPSON
Left: Seawater boils over a scour platform near Teahwhit Head. TOM TILL

Facing page: Third Beach, Olympic National Park. The "headstones" of Giant's Graveyard appear beyond Taylor Point. Composed of Hoh formation sandstones, Giant's Graveyard characterizes the North Coast's forbidding shore. PAT O'HARA

Third Beach. BOB & IRA SPRING

Facing page: Upturned sandstone beds near Rialto Beach, Olympic National Park. Tectonic forces that gave rise to the Olympic Mountains are also revealed along the coast.
PAT O'HARA

missed turn. Five minutes passed. The machinery had broken down....The auxiliary was brought into play and droned a sister sound as sweet, a blast of patient triumph."

Having found the island in the fog only delivered the party to the next of their labors—gaining admission to the storm-bound redoubt through a maze of surging channels amid the island's treacherous reefs. Dawson continues:

"And now, beneath the siren, came the hushed murmur of water,—fretful, troubled water; hissing, angry water; gnashing, frenzied water; for simultaneous with the first glimpse of the hindered light from the lofty tower, came the revelation of black reefs, at which the waters yelped and tore like angry wolves....Once we ventured into a tortuous channel, and threaded our way for a hundred yards through an inferno of black rocks lit up by the pale evil of phosphorescence, only to find ourselves confronted at last by a blank wall ashore. Out again through the horror with the instinct of fatuity, and on feverishly with the search. On and ever on! Suddenly...the keel grated on gravel, and in a moment we were comfortably on the shore of Destruction Island at 11 p.m."

From his visit to Destruction, Dawson witnessed the nightly comings and goings of rhinoceros auklets and Leach's storm-petrels. His observations made on the flat-topped upland remnant, three miles distant from land, as well as those made during the remainder of the journey, gave science its first glimpse of the wildlife treasures of the wild Olympic coast. Returning a year later with another noted ornithologist, Professor Lynds Jones of Oberlin College, Dawson made a thorough survey of the species encountered on the rough islets and completed his overall population estimate. His studies revealed that more than 100,000 seabirds nested among the Olympiades, by far the largest nesting colonies of the state.

Inland from the coast, other resources of the region also were attracting attention. The Dodwell-Rixon survey of the Olympic Forest Reserve had announced the rich forests—particularly spruce—of the remote coastal lowlands. With the creation of the reserve in 1897 by President Grover Cleveland, the land and its timber had become property of the United States government, and therefore, closed to settlement and wanton exploitation by wood-hungry timber barons. In a surprising report by the Land Office in 1901, the land was declared "not worth preserving," its timber worth less than the farm land that it obscured. President McKinley eliminated the best coastal timberlands from the Reserve, supposedly to allow agricultural development. In reality, 170,000 acres passed, in the words of an outraged Gifford Pinchot, head of the newly created Division of Forestry, "promptly and fraudulently into the hands of lumbermen." What particularly irked Pinchot and others was that these lands were claimed under the Timber and Stone Act and had been sworn as valuable for timber and "not fit for agriculture."

Nevertheless, widespread logging was still greatly hampered by the remoteness of the region and inaccessibility of its forest resources. Actual homesteading did take place in the river valleys and among the natural prairies that dotted the forest-cloaked region. One homesteader, Lars Ahlstrom, took up a claim on open, rolling bracken-covered terrain between Ozette Lake and Cape Alava in 1902. His was, according to records, the westernmost homestead in the conterminous 48 states. The Ahlstrom

71

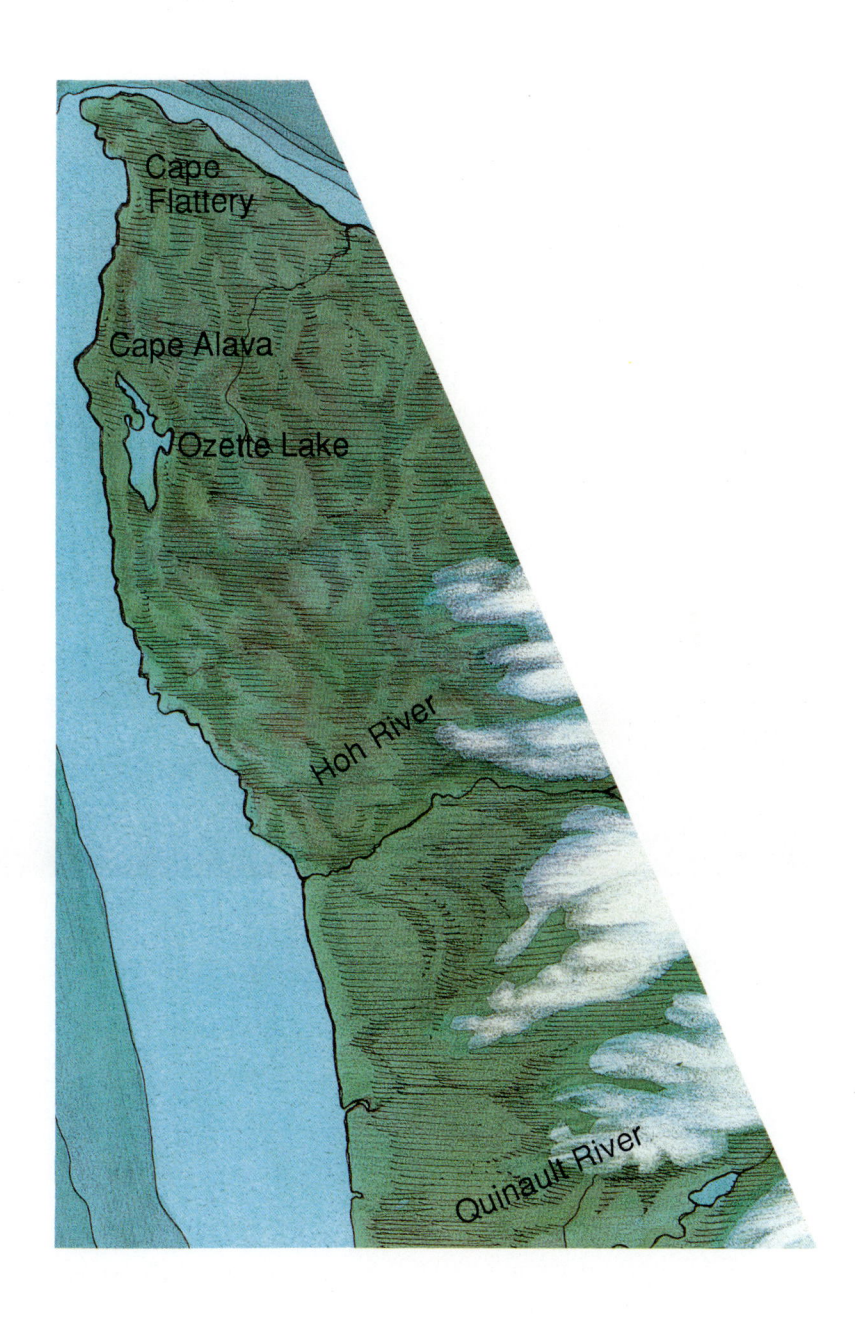

The James Island group off La Push.
BOB & IRA SPRING

homestead is now remembered as Ahlstrom's Prairie, a broad opening in the otherwise dense coastal forest traversed by a puncheon trail that leads to the ocean. Ahlstrom was only one of many Scandinavian settlers that homesteaded the Ozette area. Danes, Swedes and Norwegians found the combination of forest and sea reminiscent of their northern homelands. Even so, the comfort of appearances and the closeness to other immigrants were often not strong enough to offset the harsh conditions of the landscape.

The "opening" of the North Coast lowland region continued gradually with the extension of roads, trails and logging railroads through the first third of the 20th century. The rivers themselves were often the best routes, with Indian canoes being the common mode of conveyance for everything from groceries to loads of hay. Early settlers who had settled deep in the river valleys of the Boga-

chiel and Hoh had to travel overland by trail—even wagon roads were an unknown luxury. To reach the town of Forks from his Hoh River homestead, "Iron Man of the Hoh" John Huelsdonk often hiked the winding ridge between the Hoh and Bogachiel valleys, forded the often-swollen Bogachiel River, traversed Indian Pass to the Calawah River, then descended it to the prairie town—a distance of just less than 40 miles. Eventually, roads advanced westward from Port Angeles. Railroads too came into being following World War I, after an ambitious effort was made to acquire spruce for wartime "aeroplane" construction. The U.S. Army's Spruce Production Division, under Col. Bryce Disque, literally carved a right-of-way out of the cliff walls lining Lake Crescent, and connected the far-flung logging camps of the coastal lowland to mills and wharves of Port Angeles and markets beyond. Although Armistice arrived before the newly-available spruce stands were accessible, the railroad—and other lines subsequently built to connect with it—opened the hidden forests of the coastal foothills to timber interests, both large and small. Lumber camps flourished in the rain country of the coast.

The road link that finally connected the North Coast country to the rest of the coast—and the world at large—was the Olympic Highway. Although the counties and state inched slowly into the forbidding country in their efforts to circle the Olympic Mountains, assistance from the federal government was not forthcoming until 1913. By 1922, a road along Lake Crescent's south shore eliminated the need for ferry boats on the lake. The last link of roadway between western Clallam County and Port Angeles was forged. Between 1924 and 1930, the crews pressed south from Forks toward Grays Harbor. Road-building machinery was barged ashore near the Hoh and Queets river mouths, then dragged along the beach at low tide. Once in the dense jungle of the coastal forest, equipment became quickly mired in the deep oozing mud. In 1931, however, the loop was completed. In terms of the country and its timber, the work had just begun. The highway link would serve the sawmills and the sightseers. The coast, impervious to frontal assault, was now open on both of its flanks.

One early sightseer whose impression of the country radically affected its destiny was President Franklin D. Roosevelt. Controversy over Olympic National Park had risen through the early '30s to a fever pitch, with conservationists split into camps for and against the establishment of a national park. Forest Service management of the Mt. Olympus National Monument was seen by some as inadequate for protecting elk and their habitat that had inspired an earlier President Roosevelt to create the monument. The Forest Service, with its emphasis on utilization of timber and other natural resources, was passionately opposed to the loss of control over what remained of the Olympics' valuable forests. The National Park Service, young, eager and with growing political support, saw an opportunity to preserve much more than elk range. Instead, it saw a wilderness that stretched up the lowland river valleys into the snow-covered peaks—a functional whole, in the form of a fragment of a sea-to-mountain-top ecosystem. Timber interests, state and local elected officials, local chambers of commerce and conservationists of all stripes joined the political tug-of-war.

In an effort to judge first-hand the merits of the issue, Roosevelt visited the Olympic Peninsula in the fall of 1937. Along the shore of Lake Crescent, in a guest cabin hurriedly prepared to accommodate his large entourage of senators, agency officials and aides, he heard arguments from all corners of sentiment. Quietly, but forcefully, he insisted that the park would be a large one. During the following days, as he toured the coastal region en route to Aberdeen, he saw clearcut after clearcut and resolved that the park would include a coastal strip and at least one river corridor that connected the coast to the interior of the range.

The resulting legislation denied him his immediate goal of including the coastal segments in Olympic National Park—compromise was required in the Senate. An amendment was allowed, however, that would let the president add areas by proclamation. By one vote, on June 29, 1938, Olympic National Park was established. The proclamation amendment gave the president a trump card to play that would prove useful in the future. Irascible Harold Ickes, the Secretary of Interior, shared the president's goal for a coastal strip and river corridor. Ickes, who was also the administrator of the Public Works Administration, established P.W.A. Project Number 723, declaring that coast lands originally included in the park proposal but lost in Senate debate on the bill, would become a public works project. Legally within his power, yet blatantly in contempt of the spirit of compromise that saw the park created, he acquired, through condemnation proceedings where necessary, park land that Congress had denied. Thus with the land under the control of the P.W.A., which he directed as Administrator, he assigned its keeping to the National Park Service, which he oversaw as Secretary of the Interior. It was Harry Truman who played the president's trump—in 1953, he added the coastal strip to Olympic National Park by presidential proclamation.

With the bulk of the coastal strip a part of the park, conservationists breathed a sigh of relief. It was short-lived however, because local commercial interests found an ally in then-Park Superintendent Fred Overly. What they proposed was a highway that would follow the coast through the park's coastal strip, effectively adding roadway to the last major piece of undeveloped coast between Canada and Mexico. Overly recalled Ickes' method of acquisition of the coastal strip and argued that it had been the Secretary's intent to construct such a highway.

Above: Common murre (Uria aalge)—*one species of many that nest on the wild North Coast, making it Washington's most significant seabird-nesting habitat.* TOM ULRICH
Left: The human presence—reflections on Man and nature—persists in petroglyphs of unknown age at Wedding Rock, near Cape Alava. KARNA ORSEN

73

Above: Surf fishing at La Push.
CINDY McINTYRE
Right: Point of Arches, Olympic National Park. KEITH D. LAZELLE

Responding to what conservation activist Polly Dyer has called Overly's "bothersome threat" of a highway, wilderness advocates who gathered in Portland for the 1956 Northwest Wilderness Conference agreed that drawing attention to the value of the wild coast would arouse support for its preservation. Eager to take up the cause was Associate Supreme Court Justice William O. Douglas, who owned a fishing retreat on the Quillayute River and who knew well the coast in its wild form. In 1958, Douglas led the first of two hikes along the wilderness coastal strip designed to influence public sentiment toward preserving the wild fragment of coastline. Other prominent conservationists were invited, including Sigurd Olson, Olaus and Mardy Murie and Howard Zahniser. Proponents of the highway proposal were also invited, but none accepted.

About 70 hikers walked from Cape Alava to Rialto Beach, reveling in the power and wonderment of the primitive landscape. As they reached the roadhead near the Quillayute River, the hikers were met by pro-highway protesters. Justice Douglas recalled later that his only response to the sign carriers who advocated the coast's despoliation was to pose several questions: "Do roads have to go everywhere? Can't we save one per cent of the woods for those who love wildness?" Douglas' sentiment held sway—the road proposals eventually faded.

More recent additions to Olympic National Park have lengthened and, in some places, widened, the coastal strip of wilderness. The addition of Shi Shi Beach extended the wilderness strip northward to the south boundary of the Makah Reservation, near Cape Flattery, and also saw Ozette Lake surrounded by national park land. In addition, 1986 legislation sponsored by U.S. Senator Daniel Evans extended the park boundary seaward, to include Flattery Rocks and Quillayute Needles National Wildlife Refuges and the intertidal zone. Indeed, nearly 80 years separate two acts designed to perpetuate the wildness of some of America's wildest coast—Theodore Roosevelt's Executive Order of 1907, creating the offshore wildlife refuges, and the 1986 Olympic National Park Boundary Adjustment enacted by Congress. The interim separating those actions has been punctuated by the dedication of four generations of ardent conservationists.

The wild face of Washington, its bold northern coast, appears now in a sharply different light than when it was viewed with the fear of the mariners who first visited it. The fogs that shrouded the perils of the coast take on a less ominous form, now that the features they conceal are better known, the land behind the coast "tamed" to the point of being mundane and familiar. To William O. Douglas, the fog gave special significance to this wilderness coast. It is a fog that swallows the whole coastline, in which "a person disappears from view at camp's edge or walks as a ghostly figure. Rocks and islands that lie offshore come and go in the swirling mist. The logs piled high along the shore assume strange and grotesque forms. Everything seems out of focus. As the ceiling moves upward, patches of fog still blur the vision, making offshore islands disappear and then come magically back into view. The place seems unreal—a part of some far-off place of mystery."

Indeed, close and far-off.

Right: Led by Associate Justice of the Supreme Court William O. Douglas, conservationists hiked the wild Olympic Coast in 1958 to draw attention to its recreational value as wilderness.
BOB & IRA SPRING
Above: Each year, hundreds of backpackers retrace the route— one of the most popular hikes in Olympic National Park.
KEITH D. LAZELLE

Sea Otters

That the sea otter *(Enhydra lutris),* once was abundant along the Washington Coast is a fact established by many accounts of trading activities of early explorers and coastal Indians. Pelts were obtained near many village sites; Indians would come alongside the traders' ships bartering the furs for fragments of iron or sheets of copper. In China, the furs brought hundreds of dollars each and a cargo was worth fortunes.

Even after the coast had been settled, sea otter pelts were collected, bringing generous payment. During the 1890s, otters were hunted from the shore with 50-calibre Sharps rifles—the same weapon used to eliminate the West's buffalo herds. Hunters at Copalis Rock and Point Grenville erected towers overlooking the surf, from which the otters could be seen hundreds of yards offshore. Each hunter would mark his bullets with a distinctive sign in order to rightfully claim the otter's body when it washed ashore. By 1900, so few sea otters were found along Washington's coast that hunting, as a commercial enterprise, ceased, although incidental kills were rewarded with payment of as much as $600 for a pelt. In 1911, the United States signed a treaty with Great Britain, Japan and Russia, forbidding the hunting of sea otters. For Washington populations, the treaty arrived too late—the animal had been hunted to extinction.

Sea otters were reintroduced to the Washington Coast in 1969 and 1970. Drawn from a sizeable population at Amchitka, in the remote Aleutian Islands, 59 animals were brought to Washington. The 1969 transplant was made at Point Grenville, the site of the largest original population. Of these, 15 apparently died of hypothermia within a few weeks of release because their pelage condition had deteriorated while they were being transported from Alaska. One more died from gunshot wounds. The 1970 transplant was made without apparent losses near the mouth of the Quillayute River, another population center for the original stocks. From these locations, the otters spread northward, favoring the rugged north coast with its complex reefs, rich invertebrate fauna and seclusion.

SEA-OTTER HUNT.

Sea otters were hunted in Washington into the early 20th century, often with buffalo rifles. By the time treaties were established to protect the sleek mammals, Washington populations were gone. FROM JAMES SWAN'S *THREE YEARS RESIDENCE IN WASHINGTON TERRITORY,* COURTESY OF SPECIAL COLLECTIONS DIVISION, UNIVERSITY OF WASHINGTON LIBRARIES

In November 1741, Vitus Bering's ship, the *St. Peter,* was wrecked on a lonely island off the Kamchatka Peninsula. Salvation came to the scurvy-ridden and starving crew (although not to the dying captain) in the form of sea otters. The diminutive mammals reportedly approached the men playfully, rubbing against their legs, even as they were being beaten to death. Nourished by the meat and clothed by the luxuriant fur, surviving crewmen eventually carred news of the "new" mammal back to Russia, unleashing a period of commercial exploitation that decimated otter populations along both the Asian and North American coasts.

Today the otters are concentrated in several areas: Destruction Island, Cape Johnson, Sand Point, the Bodelteh Islands, Ozette Island and Cape Alava, well offshore and among the kelp beds. Here they feed on sea urchins, crabs, octopus and other molluscs. Limited evidence suggests that the animals migrate somewhat, with concentrations shifting seasonally between the Cape Alava and Cape Johnson sites.

Although the transplanted otters have broadened their range to include specific localities all along the coast between Destruction Island and Cape Flattery, the population has grown only slightly in size. Current estimates, based on documented sightings and aerial surveys, place the population at between 60 and 70 individuals. This apparent stagnation puzzles researchers, who casually note a sizeable annual crop of pups—15 in 1986. Factors that limit the growth of the population are presently unknown, but could include great white shark predation, storm surge mortality and the availability of food. Basic questions about the population—sex ratio of adults, reliable mortality and fecundity figures—remain unanswered. Of equal uncertainty is the status of the population as a gene pool: Are there enough individuals in this isolated group of sea otters from which to perpetuate a population with adequate genetic diversity?

The wild coast of Washington has seen many comings and goings, alterations of its cultures and nature that may, or may not, respond to the best intentions of its 20th century inhabitants. The sea otter, at play in the kelp through countless generations prior to the arrival of whites, was lost, then restored to its place in the natural ecosystem. Although the otter is present and visible to the dedicated observer, its future is not particularly secure. We have made the token gesture of releasing a few wild otters into an environment that remains wild, yet even that effort may prove futile if we have misunderstood the natural requirements of a true, working population or the complexities entailed in preserving a dynamic habitat.

Sea otters (Enhydra lutris) *transplanted on the Washington coast in 1969 and 1970 were drawn from populations at Amchitka, in the Aleutian Islands. But scientists are divided over whether Washington's original population was more closely related to present-day California populations* (above—TOM AND PAT LEESON) *or to the Aleutian stocks* (left—TOM ULRICH).

CHAPTER SIX

THE SOUTH COAST

CINDY McINTYRE

North Head and the broad expanse of the Long Beach Peninsula.
BOB & IRA SPRING

The light wears a tarnish, the uniform shade of mists hanging close to the land and water. Directionless, colorless and expressionless, it spans the entire range of hues from gray to gray. All day, the drizzle has been persistent, rising at times to bursts, driven by squally winds from the southwest. The droplets would sting if you could feel them hit—but bare skin is numb. It is afternoon, yet no crack appears on the horizon, to be wedged open by the falling light. No blaze of horizontal rays charges the scene with visual current. The oncoming darkness is arriving unannounced; the light is simply vanishing, like air from a tire with a slow leak.

The day is November 11, a day similar in its appearance to the November 11 described by Meriwether Lewis in 1805: "The wind was still high from the southwest, and drove the waves against the shore with great fury; the rain too fell in torrents, and not only drenched us to the skin, but loosened the stones on the hillsides, which then came rolling down upon us. In this comfortless situation we remained all day, wet, cold, with nothing but dried fish to satisfy our hunger; the canoes in one place, the baggage in another, and all the men scattered on floating logs, or sheltering themselves in the crevices of the rocks and hillsides." Worn from crossing the continent, the Corps of Discovery was situated at the mouth of the Columbia, wet and obviously miserable. Their goal was met, the broad Pacific was in their faces—the south coast of what was to become Washington State had been reached by a journey overland across the North American continent.

The meeting place of the Columbia with the Pacific is a place of convergence. Lewis' southwest wind converges upon the stark basalt outcrop of Cape Disappointment. Tidal whirlpools converge with the flow of the river in eddies. At the rip, meeting currents give off a sound like that of paper being crumpled. The salmon converge here, to begin their act of return to the great river and its lesser tributaries. Steamships converge here, lining up on the alternating red and white lighthouse beacon of Cape Disappointment. Off North Jetty, sooty shearwaters and black-legged kittiwakes wheel over the water; brown pelicans, like giant airborne reptiles, flog the wind with oversized wings and glide improbably. And spread out to the north, the white beaches line the low earth, expanses of sand separating the breaking surf from windrow dunes.

To describe the Washington Coast between the Quinault and Columbia Rivers with a word is easy. Its guiding theme is confluence. Its shore is a shore of beaches, born by accretion, an additive process of water-placed sediments. What water leaves, wind pushes landward. The wave undulations of the sea solidify on the land in the dune-forms of the backshore. Unlike the North Coast, where the sea has scrubbed the coast clean of sediment litter, the South Coast seems broad, generous and growing. It is a region of estuaries—Willapa Bay (once known as Shoalwater Bay; the name was changed for the sake of commerce) and Grays Harbor. It is a region of rivers swollen with tidewater, of mudflats, eelgrass and oysters. It is a

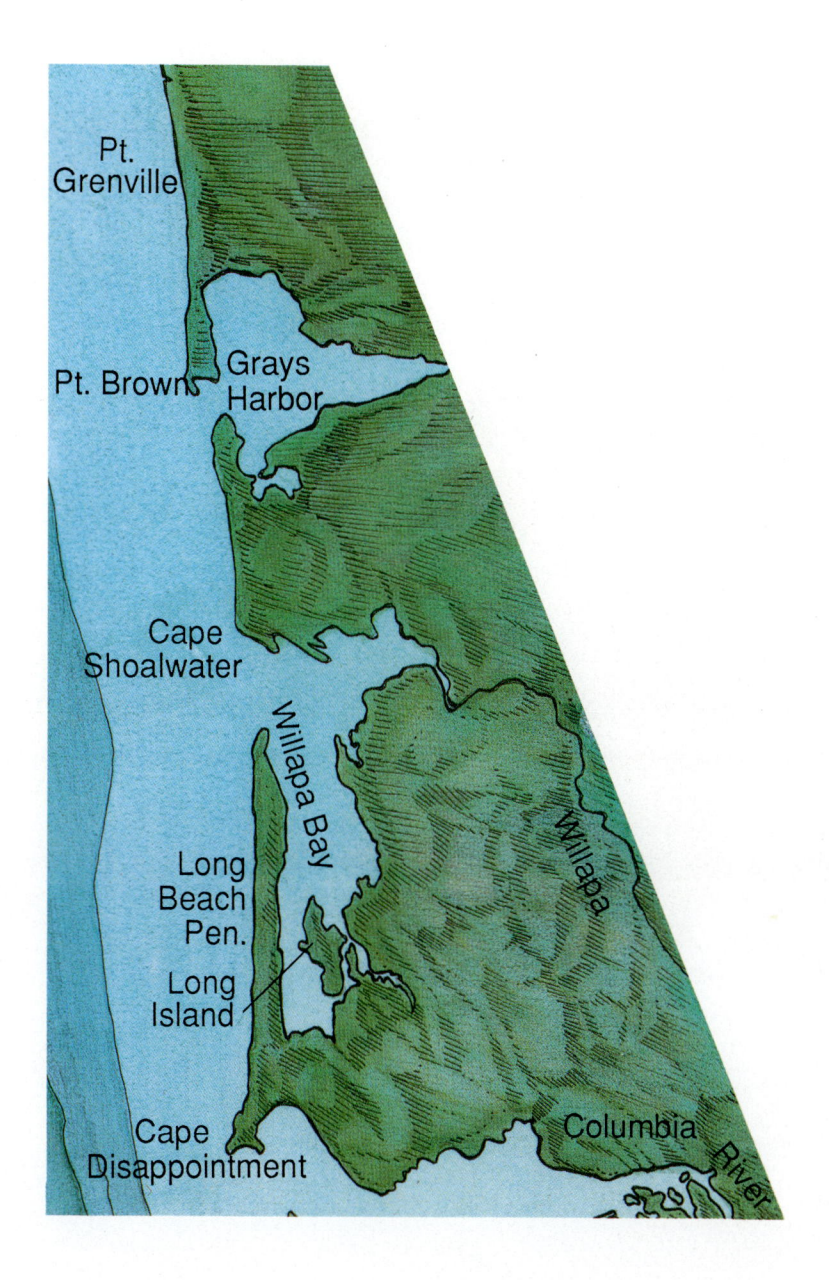

TIM THOMPSON

region teeming with waterfowl and shorebirds that congregate by the million, living currents in the great migratory surge that seasonally pours along the Pacific flyway.

Before the arrival of whites, the region was central in the commerce of Native Americans. Chinook jargon, the polyglot tongue employed by Indians as far apart as the Columbia Basin, Vancouver Island and the Southern Oregon Coast, radiated from the Lower Columbia river region in its influence—even before the arrival of whites. Coastwise trading and exchange with interior tribes promoted the free flow of tradition, slaves and material goods among Indians of the coastal region—the river and the coast were the media of this cultural fluidity. The arrival of whites as trading partners added more words to the Chinook lexicon as English and French were folded around native sounds and a wealth of new objects required description. Diverse cultural and language traditions coalesced in the South Coast river/sea/landscape.

As with the Strait of Juan de Fuca, rumors of a River of the West aroused the curiosity of early sea explorers. The 1775 voyage of Hecata brought him to a cape he called San Roque, guarding an embayment he called Bahia de la Asuncion. Although appearances hinted at the presence of a large river, he did not cross the bar and thus failed to confirm the presence of the fabled stream. In 1788, the southward leg of a trading cruise brought English merchant John Meares to the coast. He named Mt. Olympus as he passed, discovered the entrance to Shoalwater Bay, giving it that name, and rounded Cape San Roque, optimistic that he could locate the river that had eluded the Spaniards. He failed, and marked his broken faith by renaming the cape "Disappointment." In his journal he added, "We can now with safety assert that no such river as that of Saint Roc exists as laid down in the Spanish chart." The River of the West, known to some as the "Oregan," remained concealed.

The full outline of the South Coast wasn't transferred from rumor to paper until 1792, when American Captain Robert Gray of the schooner *Columbia Rediviva* located two more major features of the region. Following a meeting with Vancouver, then charting the Strait of Juan de Fuca, Gray stayed close to the coast and entered a large bay he called Bulfinch's Harbor. It was later renamed "Gray's Harbor" in his honor. Five days later, on May 11, he successfully navigated the bar at the entrance to the alternately suspected and doubted great river, naming it

"Columbia" after his vessel. According to pioneer Washington historian Edmond S. Meany these discoveries were critical to the success of claims later made by the fledgling United States over territory in the Northwest. Gray lingered inside the river's entrance long enough to chart features of the lower river and visit an Indian village located at the present site of Chinook, a site that would later be visited by the Lewis and Clark expedition.

Further exploration of the Columbia River mouth, Shoalwater Bay and Grays Harbor continued sporadically. Vancouver, having missed his opportunity on the northward leg of his journey, returned after circling what is now Vancouver Island and ordered the storeship *Daedalus* to chart Gray's Harbor, while the *Discovery* and *Chatham* proceeded to the Columbia River. The *Chatham* successfully crossed the bar and ventured about 20 miles upriver. The ship's boats successfully explored another 80 miles of the river before returning downstream and crossing the tempestuous bar to open sea.

Subsequent surveys of Grays Harbor and the Columbia River mouth were made by the United States Exploring Expedition under the command of Lieutenant Charles Wilkes in 1841. Ironically, this expedition to chart the Columbia mouth, along with other harbors on the Northwest Coast, dramatically revealed the need for detailed knowledge of the perilous river mouth. On Sunday, July 18, the sloop-of-war *Peacock* lurched to a dead stop off Cape Disappointment. Fast in the sand, she was abandoned and, within 24 hours, destroyed by the force of rolling combers. The wreck of the *Peacock* was the ninth recorded; most of the others had occurred while the fated vessels groped over the bar attempting to take soundings and locate a channel. The *Peacock's* loss gave one of its passengers, James D. Dana, the expedition's geologist, a close look at the forces working at the great river's mouth. His description of river bar formation processes later made its way into his monumental *Manual of Geology:*

"The material of the sand-bars which obstruct the entrances of harbors has two main sources: an inner, and outer; the former fluvial, the latter the wave-and-current driftings of the coast, which contribute so largely to sand-barriers. The positions of the bars depend much on the strength of the river current; but also on the direction, form, and supplies of the wave-and-current movement produced by the storm-winds....The depth of water over

The Columbia River mouth was charted at great cost to the United States Exploring Expedition under the command of Lieutenant Charles Wilkes, in 1841. The loss of the sloop-of-war Peacock *was a blow to the expedition; the shoal upon which it grounded retains the name Peacock Spit. Wilkes' chart was short-lived in its usefulness, however; within five years the shifting bar had rendered the chart obsolete.* U.S. COAST AND GEODETIC SURVEY

CRANBERRIES

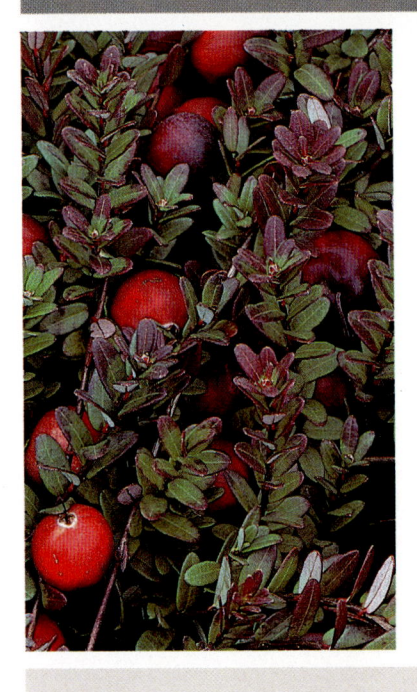

Left to right: Vaccinium macrocarpon—*the "Thanksgiving berry"—an important cash crop in areas of Pacific and Grays Harbor counties. Berries redden on ground-hugging shrubs and are harvested using a float technique or, as was common before mechanization, dryland picking.*

Pil ollalie to the Indians, "the ruby of the bog" to its growers—the cranberry enjoys unique status as a necessary seasonal condiment, a beverage fruit of increasing popularity, and an agricultural cash crop ideally suited to "unproductive" bog habitats of Washington's south coast region.

Indians and settlers of Shoalwater Bay country took advantage of native cranberries *(Vaccinium oxycoccus)* that grew in the bogs of water perched on beds of peat that are common in Pacific County. Some have attributed the healthfulness of local Indians to the abundant source of winter-time vitamin C. Small, native berries were never successfully cultivated, but out of curiosity and later, determined enterprise, several pioneers made efforts to introduce varieties of Eastern berries to a landscape that bore striking similarities to berry-growing regions of New England.

Anthony Chabot is credited with being the first to successfully culture eastern berries *(Vaccinium macrocarpon)* on the Long Beach Peninsula. In partnership with three other businessmen, he acquired 1,200 acres between 1872 and 1877, developed and planted bogs, and in 1883, harvested his first crop.

Chabot's bog produced berries until the 1890s. Harvesting was performed by hand by field crews of Indians, Chinese, women and children. Chabot's early success encouraged a few others, but combined factors of limited seasonal markets, distance to markets, slow return on capital investment and bad planting stock hampered the growth of cranberry culture.

Although the profitability of cranberry farming was marginal during the years of its infancy, speculation on potential cranberry cropland proved lucrative. Through the decade of the 1910s, holding companies bought up thousands of acres of Long Beach Peninsula marshland, promising big profits to investors who could "devote the combined energy of capital, scientific knowledge and perfect natural resources." The "big profits" went to the speculators—would-be growers went broke. Disease, frost and imperfect growing methods held the upper hand.

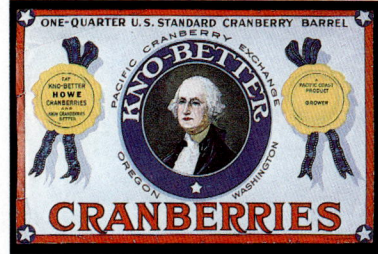

Relief arrived in the 1920s, with the establishment of a cranberry research station, operated by D.J. Crowley of the State College of Washington. Crowley studied the climate and soils of the region and diseases and pests of the berry, and slowly discovered farming methods best suited to Washington's coast. Experimenting with a wide array of cranberry varieties, early chemical pesticides and frost-protection methods, he complemented the advances being made by growers who improved methods of harvesting the succulent red fruit. Crowley's long career as Washington's cranberry expert and the coming of age of Pacific Northwest cranberry culture spanned the same time period.

The marketing of cranberries also matured through the years. Early growers had made attempts to work cooperatively to sell their berries. Following a 1941 fire that destroyed their cannery, the Grays Harbor-Pacific County growers merged with the Cranberry Canners Company, an east coast cooperative formed in Massachusetts in 1930. By 1946, the co-op had become the National Cranberry Association and in 1959, changed its name to Ocean Spray Cranberries Inc. Through Ocean Spray, Washington growers have seen their market expand to include all of the western states except California. The "Thanksgiving berry" has become a year-round staple in the forms of juice and processed products.

FACING PAGE, LEFT: KEITH D. LAZELLE; CENTER AND RIGHT, BRUCE HANDS. THIS PAGE, LEFT: ILWACO HERITAGE CENTER; TOP AND BOTTOM, KARNA ORSEN.

the sand-bars at the mouth of a large river or bay is, in great part, only 3 to 10 feet: a remarkable fact, considering the opposing forces at work—the tidal outflow and inflow, and the plunge of the storm-made waves over the mobile sands. The sands lie along the area of rest between the contesting movements."

Dana's close observation of these phenomena was interesting in the pursuit of science but costly in terms of the loss of the vessel—"the old craft that had been home for three eventful years" of the Wilkes Expedition. Even that hard-won intelligence soon became obsolete owing to the dynamic nature of the bar. Only five years later, Lieutenant Neil M. Howison, commanding the schooner *Shark,* noted that "the sands about the mouth of the Columbia had undergone great changes within a short time past, and that a spit had formed out to the eastward from the spot upon with the *Peacock* was wrecked in 1841, which made it impossible to enter the river by the old marks, or those laid down on Wilkes' chart." The *Shark* grounded briefly on her inbound passage, and was wrecked on her outbound crossing of the bar.

It was decades before jetties on the north and south sides of the river mouth were constructed to force the river current to scour out sand deposits deep enough to allow safe passage through one channel, 2,500 feet in width. A lighthouse to mark treacherous Cape Disappointment was not as long in the making. An 1848 survey of the lighthouse sites on the West Coast and considerable political pressure resulted in the establishment of the Cape Disappointment light 220 feet above the churning water. Its introduction to service in 1856 came only after several delays—one caused by the wreckage of the *Oriole,* carrying supplies for the light's construction; another, of two years' duration, while the empty tower awaited its beacon.

While the Columbia's mouth was eventually tamed, the effects of that taming radically altered the form of other parts of the South Coast, particularly the Long Beach Peninsula. The construction of the North Jetty had a profound influence on the longshore drift regime at the river's mouth. Sediments entering the ocean were no longer subject to the relatively equal forces of tidal current and ocean surge waves that held them at the bar. By narrowing the river mouth channel and increasing the river velocity, sediments were flushed into the nearshore zone where prevailing currents swept them northward. This redistribution of sediments has resulted in the addition of as much as 4,000 acres of land to the Long Beach Peninsula over an 80-year period. In the Long Beach-Seaview area, this accretion has added over 1,200 feet to the width of the beach.

Shoalwater Bay went unexplored in a formal sense until 1852, when it was surveyed by Lieutenant Alden, of the U.S. Coast Survey. However, settlement of the region was already well underway, spreading northward from the Columbia mouth. Isolated habitations were dotted along the uneven shore, near the mouths of rivers like the Naselle, Nemah and Palix. This era of Shoalwater pioneer history was well documented by James G. Swan in his book *The Northwest Coast or, Three Years'* *Residence in Washington Territory,* published in 1857. Swan, whom we know from a large body of writing generated during his long tenure at Neah Bay and Port Townsend, was a New Englander briefly attracted by the glimmer of the California goldfields. His arrival in Shoalwater country in 1852 came about as a result of the brisk commerce between Shoalwater Bay and San Francisco in logs and oysters. The dark forests of towering spruce, fir and cedar that lined the shores and the rich shoals of native oysters that covered the broad estuary held a wealth of commodities needed to shelter and feed legions of California gold-seekers.

The native oysters did not long survive; their harvest could be likened only to mining itself. Following the first shipment of 1,000 bushels, made in 1850, oystering was a booming industry. Towns of Bay Center, Bruceport, and Oysterville were founded around oyster harvesting. Beds were staked and picked, and the little native bivalves were shipped by the schooner-load to San Francisco. By the 1880s, the native oyster fishery was in decline—by 1910, the native oysters had largely disappeared. Subsequent introductions of other species—Chesapeake oysters around 1900, and Japanese oysters in 1924—restored commercial oystering to the bay. The eastern oysters flourished for about two decades before disease and unknown factors caused their decline. Japanese oysters remain a significant resource today with annual harvests valued at about $2 million.

The negative effects of the dynamic interplay between shore and currents are revealed at Cape Shoalwater, the northerly point of land at the entrance to Willapa Bay. Here, the channel at the bay's entrance has migrated

Left: Treacherous sands near the Columbia River mouth have claimed many vessels including the French barque Alice—*laden with 3,000 tons of cement. The 1909 wreck occurred at North Beach.* PRENTIS PHOTO, PAT ASLIN COLLECTION, ILWACO HERITAGE CENTER
The wreck of the Catala, *at the Grays Harbor entrance.* BOB & IRA SPRING

Facing page:
Cape Disappointment Light. Stripes on the tower and alternating red and white signals from the beacon distinguish Disappointment from North Head, its close neighbor.
CINDY McINTYRE

Above: Willapa Bay estuary. Of the 254 species of birds seen on Willapa National Wildlife Refuge, 86 use the refuge for nesting. SCOTT PRICE
Right: A narrow-gauge railroad served the tourist meccas of the Long Beach Peninsula between 1889 and 1930. PAT ASLIN COLLECTION, ILWACO HERITAGE CENTER

northward, resulting in dramatic erosion of low-lying beach and dune shorelands. Estimates place the advance of the sea at approximately 100 feet per year—the most severe on the Pacific Coast. In human terms, the loss of the cape has forced the relocation of the Willapa Bay light, a major state highway and a pioneer cemetery. Recent evidence suggests that the rate of erosion is decreasing—nevertheless planners and property owners watch the sea's "progress" with concern.

Grays Harbor (the possessive apostrophe is not used in the contemporary place-name) represents the drowned extension of the broad Chehalis River valley. During the period that continental glaciers choked the Puget lowland, much of the runoff drained toward the sea through what is now the Chehalis River valley, resulting in an enormous drainway. For a short time, the Chehalis was a silty river moving as much water as the modern-day Columbia. As the currents surged through the lowland, large quantities of gravel and silt also were deposited, resulting in the soils now characteristic of that region. As the glaciers melted, the runoff slowed and, over the millenia, the sea rose. Slowly overcoming the lowland, the water backed up into the Chehalis Valley, creating the long tongue of ocean that we see now. Points to the north and south of the harbor entrance—Point Brown to the north and Point Chehalis to the south—formed relatively recently, as longshore sediments were deposited to form sandspits.

The ongoing effort required to keep the shipping channels of Grays Harbor free of accumulating sediment attests to the natural reclamation process underway in the estuary. Sediments, many dislodged from the foothills of the southern Olympics and northern Willapa Hills by logging and intensive roadbuilding, wash into the bay with each freshet, contributing to a geologic process that will eventually see the filling of the entire estuary basin. The increase of sediment deposition that has occurred in the historical era also has resulted in significant modification of marine plant and animal communities found between the entrance to Grays Harbor and Point Grenville, to the north. Pioneer sea otter hunters frequently referred to a 20-mile-long kelp bed as an area rich with the sleek furbearers. No sign remains now of such a kelp bed—the rocky substrate upon which it thrived is now buried by sediment.

The beaches between Grays Harbor and the Quinault River begin to show the form, so visible farther north, of alternating headlands and cusp beaches. River sediments from the Chehalis River join the flow of fine particles that are transported along the coast and laid on the gently sloping shore. These beaches are broad and expansive, and backed by low dunes.

The present-day economies of towns of the south coast hinge on another sort of confluence that dominates the region, that of visitors who seasonally flock to the broad beaches for the many forms of recreation that the coast affords. Ilwaco and Westport host large numbers of recreational anglers, who dutifully rise before dawn, and swallow their eye-opening coffee and breakfast in cafes that line the wharves where the charter boats dock. Salmon, bottomfish and albacore tuna are the main attractions, but watching day break on the rolling swells has its own rewards.

Tourism on the Long Beach Peninsula has been an economic mainstay for nearly a century. The Ilwaco, Shoalwater Bay & Grays Harbor Railroad was formed in 1883 in order to form a link between Ilwaco and Oysterville on the peninsula. By 1889, a narrow-gauge railroad was in operation between the wharf at Ilwaco and Nahcotta, on Shoalwater Bay. Tourists arriving by steamboat from Astoria and Portland transferred to the waiting train and were carried to resort destinations that lined the peninsula. Towns of Seaview, Long Beach, Oceanside, Klipsan Beach and Ocean Park grew as colorful and busy centers of commerce catering to the needs of the seasonal influx of visitors.

Coastal beaches north of Grays Harbor also have attracted waves of tourists, although the trend developed more recently there than at Long Beach. Ocean Shores, on wind- and wave-swept Point Brown, north of the Grays Harbor entrance, remains one of the fastest developing resort areas of the Washington Coast, following aggressive promotion in the 1950s and 1960s.

The south coast remains a swirl of many forces—physical, biological, economic and cultural—that give Washington's coast its unique identity. The Columbia River, Grays Harbor and Willapa Estuary, as features of that coast, gave Native Americans, explorers and settlers a foothold that admitted civilization. It came early and stayed long. This coastal quarter continues to attract people. Its accessibility to both Puget Sound and Portland metropolitan populations and the characteristic flavor of its generous beaches, cottage-littered resort towns and public pleasure-grounds have always made it a vacation destination with broad demographic appeal. Timber from the foothills, oysters from the estuaries, salmon funneling toward the rivers, berries in the bogs and a variety of other resources continue to sustain descendants of pioneers and newcomers who have chosen to remain in south coast country. They understand well the significance of factors that converge in their rich environment and view with skepticism changes that would alter the region's diverse resource base and distinctive character. Change is constant here, marked in natural cycles—rhythms of tide and current, the wanderings of migrating birds and fish, the seasons of heavy winter rains and light summer fogs. Against such cycles as these, the powerful confluence of history and place shapes a unity not unlike a featureless and overcast November sky.

Fresh salt air always has attracted throngs. Coastal pleasuring grounds at Joe Creek, Pacific Beach Woods, catered to car campers in 1924.
HISTORICAL PHOTO COURTESY OF JONES PHOTO CO., ABERDEEN, WA

OYSTERVILLE

Above: Oyster harvesting in 1910.
SPECIAL COLLECTIONS DIV., UNIV. OF WASHINGTON LIBRARIES

*Facing page, clockwise from top: The heirloom rose, "Dorothy Perkins," graces the Tom Crellin House, built in 1869.
The Oysterville Church, centerpiece of the Oysterville National Historic district, was built in 1892.
The R.H. Espy House, built in 1871 by Robert Espy, Oysterville's co-founder.*
BRUCE HANDS PHOTOS

Winter clouds hang low over the wide expanse of bay, giving an even shade of light to the scene. It is not raining, but a squall passed recently and every surface, including the snowberries, glistens wet. Gusts of fresh wind press at the grasses and on the bleached cannery a loose piece of corrugated metal works against its fastenings with each blast. Weathered pilings stick out of the mud like bones. The view is spare; warm earthy tones of dry sedge and pale dune rye give way to the deep chocolate of bay mud that extends far into the distance. This is Oysterville's view of its estuary, the fertile bay that gave the town its life and has since taken some back.

To turn around and view the town from the bay is to see its face (what are now the fronts of the houses from the road were their original backs). Chimney smoke lies out flat against the blue silhouettes of the forest backdrop. A dozen houses are at least partly visible, enclosed in shrubs and yard trees. A few have picket fences.

Born as a seafood larder for California's hungry miners in 1854, Oysterville, by rights, should be gone now. Most of the towns founded with it are. Its native oysters vanished long ago, picked clean out. Its saloons and hotels quieted long ago and faded away. Most of its sons and daughters have long since found promise elsewhere. A few of its families remain, along with a handful of its houses, some decorated in gingerbread trim and fresh paint, others weedbound and sagging. In Oysterville, time and the bay show their marks, but the greater part of civilization does not. Its position near the end of the Long Beach Peninsula hasn't been a stopping point on the way to anywhere since bay steamers quit transferring passengers many decades ago. Unless you intend specifically to visit Oysterville, chances are you won't.

Yet for all of its isolation and bygone splendor, Oysterville attracts visitors. It would be entirely fair to say that the town enjoys a renaissance that few other communities of the coast can claim. Not because of some economic development scheme, or fast-buck theme hype. Visitors don't come to look at illusion, they come instead to squint into time, to see a community that remains in appropriate scale with its past, honest with itself.

On July 4, 1976, Oysterville was dedicated as a National Historic District, an 80-acre site containing 12 houses and two public buildings (a school and a church) built before 1910; 14 or 15 buildings constructed in the 1920s; and three or four "new" houses. "New" means they were built since 1935. The dedication followed nearly four years of effort by Dale Espy Little, granddaughter of one of the town's founders, Robert H. Espy.

Espys have had a stake in Oysterville since Chief Nahcati showed Robert Espy the wealth of oysters that grew on the unsettled side of Shoalwater Bay in 1854. A town bloomed, many of its buildings constructed out of redwood lumber used to ballast the empty oyster schooners on their trip from San Francisco. When the oysters failed, Espys remained. Those who left returned periodically, drawn by family gatherings and the natural magnetism of scenes unchanged, faithful to memories.

Those memories went public with Willard Espy's *Oysterville: Roads to Grandpa's Village*, published in 1977. The book formed a roadmap through the private history that led to the town's founding. Some say the book made the Espys everybody's pioneer family. If so, the efforts of Willard's sister Dale to preserve the historical site made Oysterville everybody's pioneer town. Today, many visitors to Oysterville know the town intimately even before they see it, and when they see it, recognition is complete.

There is some quality in Oysterville that lets it be the sum of more than 130 years of history on Washington's Coast. It retains its human presence in correct proportion to its natural setting. It reveals what allegiance to a place can offer as rewards. It affords an intangible continuity, where past and future blend, where generations visit but leave few marks. Oysterville persists in part because its preservation threatened no grander development; ambition had moved on. What it left was the elegance of an earlier time preserved to shape its future.

89

Place Names on the Washington Coast

compiled by Sheila Sandiford

Abbey Island (North Coast). The heavily eroded rock island was named in 1866 by a U.S. Coast Survey because of its seeming resemblance to an ancient abbey.

Aberdeen (South Coast). This city at the mouth of the Chehalis and Wishkah rivers was named for Aberdeen, Scotland, by B.A. Seaborg, who established a fish-packing plant there. It originally was dubbed Wishkah in 1867 by founder Samuel Benn.

Baada Point (Strait of Juan de Fuca). Site of a former Makah Indian fishing village, it originally was named Mecena Point in 1841 by Cmdr. Charles Wilkes of the Wilkes Expedition. The present name appeared in the 1852 U.S. Coast Survey as Baadah Point.

Bahobohosh Point (North Coast). The original Makah Indian name has been retained for this rocky point on Mukkaw Bay.

Baker Bay (South Coast). In 1792, Lt. W.R. Broughton of the Vancouver Expedition named this large circular bay near the Columbia River mouth for Capt. James Baker of the brig *Jenny*, which was at anchor there when Broughton arrived. It also has been known as Haley's Bay, Deception Bay and Rogue's Harbor.

Beckett Point (Strait). Capt. Henry Kellett chose the present name in 1846, saying it was the local name for an extensive, fortified Indian village here. It had been named Sandy Point in 1841 by Cmdr. Charles Wilkes, and was known to early settlers as Ft. Point after the Indian fortification.

Bogachiel River (North Coast). The Indian name of this 40-mile river, *Bo-qua-tchiel*, means "muddy after rain."

Cannonball Island (North Coast). So named for its sandstone concretions. The island's original Makah name was *wa'h-yeah-iq*, and warriors staged games there aimed at improving their accuracy with bow and arrow.

Cape Alava (North Coast). Originally dubbed *Punta de Hijosa* by Manuel Quimper on Aug. 6, 1790, this most westerly point in Washington State later appeared on Spanish charts as *Punta de Alava* for Jose Manuel de Alava, naval commandant at Acapulco in Mexico. Capt. Henry Kellett charted it as Point Alava in 1847.

Cape Disappointment (South Coast). Capt. John Meares named the cape July 6, 1788, after failing to locate the Columbia River at a point charted in 1775 by Bruno de Heceta.

Cape Flattery (Strait). Charted by Capt. James Cook of the British Navy on March 22, 1778, this is the oldest name—other than the Pacific Ocean—now in use on maps of the state. The cape flattered Cook with the hope of a passage between it and an island beyond (Vancouver Island). But he failed to find the Strait of Juan de Fuca due to bad weather, and discounted its existence. Other early explorers called it Cape Claaset or Cape Classet, after the Indian name, Klasset, and *Punta de Martinez*.

Picking cranberries at Morden's Marsh (1935 ?). COURTESY OF MRS. D.J. CROWLEY, PROVIDED BY THE PICTURE ATTIC, LONG BEACH, WA

Cape George (Strait). In 1841, Cmdr. Charles Wilkes named the cape East Bluff. But in 1846, Capt. Henry Kellett of the Royal Navy renamed it in honor of Capt. George Vancouver.

Cape Johnson (North Coast). Records showing which Johnson was responsible for the cape's name apparently have not survived; the name was very common in pioneer days. The Quileute Indian name was *Ta-qwa-at*, meaning "big curve in the bay."

Cape Shoalwater (South Coast). The descriptive name was given on July 5, 1788, by John Meares. Other names used previously were Cape Foulweather and Point Lewis.

Carr Point (Strait). In 1790, Manuel Quimper placed a cross there but did not name the point; In 1792, Capt. George Vancouver refitted ships at the point but likewise did not name it. In 1841, Cmdr. Charles Wilkes named it Carr's Point after Lt. Overton Carr of his expedition, and a shortened version survives. The local name, Contractors Point, appears on some maps.

Clallam Bay (Strait). The bay was entered on British Admiralty Charts as Clallam in 1846 by Capt. Henry Kellett. It is an anglicized version of the Indian tribal name, *S'klah-lam,* meaning "big, strong nation." The Indian name for this bay was *Kla-kla-wice*. A village on the eastern shore takes its name from Clallam Bay.

Copalis Head (South Coast). Named for the Indian term for the area, *Che-pa-lis,* meaning "opposite the rock." An offshore rock bears the name Copalis, as do a nearby river and community.

Crane Point (Strait). The Wilkes Expedition named this feature Middle Point; the current name is of local origin and has been in use since the 1890s.

Destruction Island (North Coast). The rocky 40-acre island was named *Isla de Dolores* by Spanish navigator Juan Francisco de Bodega y Quadra on July 14, 1775, after six of his men were killed by Indians near Point Grenville. The men had gone ashore for water.

Discovery Bay (Strait). Important in the early development of the state, the bay was explored in 1790 by Manuel Quimper and used as a base by Juan Francisco de Eliza in 1791. In 1792, Capt. George Vancouver also used it as a base, and on May 2, 1792, named it for his flagship, *Discovery*.

Grays Harbor Veneer Plant, 1924.
COURTESY OF JONES PHOTO CO., ABERDEEN, WA

Dungeness River (Strait). A 32-mile river, spit, bay, harbor and community all bear the same name. Capt. George Vancouver initially named the nearby spit and bay it encloses New Dungeness, after a promontory on the Strait of Dover. All but the bay now bear the present, shortened name. One arm of the sandy, 5-mile spit is called Graveyard Spit because 30 Haida Indians were buried there in 1875 after a massacre by Clallam Indians.

Eagle Point (Strait). During pioneer days, it was named for a conspicuous eagle nest in a high tree here.

Ediz Hook (Strait). The 3-mile spit was named in 1846 by Capt. Henry Kellett, who anglicized the name of a fortified Clallam Indian village there, *Yennis,* meaning "good place." In the 1850s, the spit was called False Dungenness.

Elwha River (Strait). Charted in 1847 by Capt. Henry Kellett, the river takes its name from the Quileute word, *E-ilth-quatl,* meaning "elk."

Father and Son Rocks (North Coast). The name for these two rocks, one large and one small, essentially is a translation of the original Makah name.

Freshwater Bay (Strait). In 1790, Lopez de Haro named the bay Ensenada de Davila for Capt. Juan Herrera Davila of the Spanish navy. Manuel Quimper of the *Princesa Real* secured a supply of fresh water there in the same year. The present name appeared first in 1847, however, on British Admiralty charts prepared by Capt. Henry Kellett.

Fuca Pillar (North Coast). In 1788, John Meares named the rocky crag Fuca's Pillar for Juan de Fuca. The Makah Indian name was *Tsar-tsar-dark,* meaning "tall, tall leaning rock." Fur traders called it Pinnacle Rock and Pinnacle Island.

Giants Graveyard (North Coast). The landmark is a rugged collection of about a dozen sea stacks and rock islands, and was first charted in May 1887 by John Francis Pratt, a coastal surveyor.

Grays Harbor (South Coast). Named after Robert Gray, who discovered the protected, navigable saltwater harbor on May 7, 1792, naming it Bullfinch's Harbor. It had been named *Puerto Grek* by Martinez y Zayas, and in 1825 was called Whitbey Harbour by David Douglas.

Green Point (Strait). The heavily wooded point was given its descriptive name in the 1854 U.S. Coast Survey.

Hoh River (North Coast). The present name is a much-simplified form of the Indian name, *Oh-la-qu-hoh* or *Hooh-oh-ah-lat,* meaning "can speak Quinault at that place." In 1787, Capt. Charles W. Barkley named it Destruction River when members of his boat crew were killed by Indians while securing fresh water. On July 14, 1775, Bodega y Quadra had lost six men in a similar experience; he called it *Rio de los Martires*.

Hoko River (Strait). In 1846, Capt. Henry Kellett charted the name as Okho, his version of the Indian name, *Ho-qwol-th.* The Indian word means "projecting," referring to a huge rock at the canyon's mouth.

Hoquiam (South Coast). This forest-products manufacturing center and a nearby river take their name from an Indian band, the *Ho-qui-umpts,* which means "hungry for wood." This refers to their custom of using river driftwood for fuel.

Humptulips River (South Coast). The name is from the Quinault word, *Ho-to-la-bixh,* meaning "hard to pole."

James Island (North Coast). In 1775, this small, U-shaped island that connects with the beach at low tide was included with Quillayute Needle under the name *Los Frayles,* given by Bruno Heceta. The present name is for Francis W. James of Port Townsend, who in 1855 became the first white man to scale the rocky island's peak.

Klachopis Point (Strait). The original Makah Indian name for this rocky ledge has been retained, although in 1841, Cmdr. Charles Wilkes named it Sail Rock Point, and in 1846, Capt. Henry Kellett charted it as Scarborough Point.

Kulakala Point (Strait). The name is based on a combination of Chinook jargon words for bird (*Kula*) and goose (*Kala*), referring to the one-time abundance of waterfowl here. In 1841, it was named Kulo Kala Point by Cmdr. Charles Wilkes.

Ox team at log dump, Grays Harbor. SPECIAL COLLECTIONS DIV., UNIV. OF WASHINGTON LIBRARIES

La Push (North Coast). The name of the Indian fishing village at the mouth of the Quillayute River is Chinook jargon, a corruption of the French *la bouche,* meaning "the mouth."

Leadbetter Point (South Coast). The name of this low, sandy point at the north end of Long Beach Peninsula originally was charted as Low Point on July 5, 1788, by Capt. John Meares. But it was changed in 1852 by Lt. James Alden of the U.S. Coast Survey to honor Lt. Danville Leadbetter, a survey associate.

Long Island (South Coast). The descriptive name of this irregular, seven-mile-long island in Willapa Bay was given in 1857 by James G. Swan.

Lyre River (Strait). In 1790, the stream was named *Rio de Cuesta* by Lopez de Haro; the same name was applied in 1791 by Juan Francisco de Eliza. In 1847, Capt. Henry Kellett charted it as River Lyre; the reversed form is used today.

McKenzie Head (South Coast). The feature was named in fur-trading days for Donald McKenzie, partner in Pacific Fur Co. and leader of the first overland party to reach Astoria, Ore., in 1811.

Miller Peninsula (Strait). The sparsely populated peninsula was named for an early settler and logger.

Moclips (South Coast). The community, at the mouth of a river of the same name, is a variation of the Quinault *No-mo-Klopish,* meaning "people of the turbulent water."

Mukkaw Bay (North Coast). The shallow bay south of Cape Flattery is spelled the way the Makah Indians pronounce their tribal name.

Nachotta (South Coast). Formerly platted on the south as Nachotta and the north as Sealand, this oyster center was named for Chief Nachotte, who guided settlers to the oyster beds.

Neah Bay (North Coast). This protected bay, and the community of the same name, take their name from a Makah chief whose actual name was *Dee-ah*. It was christened Neah Bay in 1847 by Capt. Henry Kellett, who simplified the chief's name. In 1792, the Spanish erected a fort here, the first structure in the state built by white men. The bay had been named *Bahia de Nunez Gaona* in 1790 by Spanish Capts. Manuel Quimper and Juan Francisco de Eliza.

North Beach Peninsula (South Coast). The 28-mile ocean beach peninsula originally was called North Peninsula, but was changed by popular consent to the more descriptive name.

Observatory Point (Strait). Capt. Henry Kellett used this point for observations in 1847, and entered this name on British Admiralty charts. Manuel Quimper named it *Punta de Salvi* on July 4, 1790.

Oyhut (South Coast). This village's name is a modification of the Chinook *Weh-hut,* meaning road, path or trail. It also is known locally as Damon, after C.A. Damon, the area's first settler who claimed land in 1861.

Oysterville (South Coast). The community was named in 1852 by I.A. Clark, an oysterman, for the abundance of native oysters in Willapa Bay. The former seat of Pacific County, its records were kidnapped in 1893 by South Bend.

Ozette Island (North Coast). The name, from the Makah Indian *O-se-ilth* or *O-se-elth,* means "middle tribe." Ozette also is the name of a small resort community, eight-mile-long lake and river.

Palix River (South Coast). The Chinook name means "slough covered with trees." One of its three forks is known locally as Tomhays River, for a notorious Indian who lived there in the 1850s. In 1857, James G. Swan referred to the stream as Palux River; another early version was the Copalus River.

Pillar Point (Strait). The descriptive name was placed on British Admiralty charts in 1847 by Capt. Henry Kellett; it was approved by the U.S. Coast Survey in 1858.

Pitship Point (Strait). The point was named in 1841 by Cmdr. Charles Wilkes for one of his crew members, although records do not indicate which one was honored.

Point Chehalis (South Coast). The present name, charted in 1841 by Cmdr. Charles Wilkes, is a modification of the Chehalis Indian word *Chikeeles,* which means "sand."

Point Damon (South Coast). Named for pioneer C.A. Damon, who settled at Oyhut. An unofficial, alternate name is Damon's Point.

Point Grenville (South Coast). The point was named April 28, 1792, by Capt. George Vancouver to honor Lord William Wyndham Grenville, then British secretary of state. In the same year, Galiano had named it *Punte de la Bastida* for its fort-like appearance; the Heceta Expedition in 1775 had called it *Punta de los Martires,* after several crew members were killed by Indians.

Point of Arches (North Coast). The descriptive name refers to huge rocks on the point which wave action has eroded into arches.

Point Wilson (Strait). Two versions are given of the name's origin: one says the point was named on June 6, 1792, by Capt. George Vancouver for Capt.

Weatherwax mill (later Anderson and Middleton), Aberdeen, circa 1880s.
WILLIAM D. JONES HISTORICAL COLLECTION, COURTESY OF JONES PHOTO CO., ABERDEEN, WA

Drying oyster shells before grinding for chicken feed, 1910. SPECIAL COLLECTIONS DIV., UNIV. OF WASHINGTON LIBRARIES, PHOTO BY A. CURTIS

George Wilson of the Royal Navy; the other states it was named by Cmdr. Charles Wilkes in 1841 for Thomas Wilson, an expedition sailmaker's mate.

Port Angeles (Strait). Capt. George Vancouver in 1792 condensed a long Spanish name for the protected bay, christened *Puerto de Neustra Senora de Los Angeles* in 1791 by Juan Francisco de Eliza. The name of a post office, established here in 1861 as Cherbourg, was changed to Port Angeles the following year. The city, fronting the harbor, is the Clallam County seat.

Protection Island (Strait). The rocky island was named on May 27, 1792, by Capt. George Vancouver because it sheltered Discovery Bay from north and northwesterly winds, and also because it could be fortified for military protection.

Quillayute River (North Coast). The apt Indian name means "joining together of rivers." The Quillayute is the confluence of the Soleduck and Bogachiel rivers. The same name, spelled Quileute, refers to the tribe whose headquarters is La Push, at the river's mouth.

Quimper Peninsula (Strait). The S-shaped peninsula was named in 1862 by Capt. George Davidson of the U.S. Coast Survey to honor Spanish explorer Manuel Quimper, who charted much of the region in 1790. It had been named the Dickerson Peninsula in 1841 by the Wilkes Expedition, to honor Mahlon Dickerson, secretary of the U.S. Navy when Wilkes Expedition orders were issued in March 1838.

Rialto Beach (North Coast). The beach is believed to have been named by area resident Alexander Conlon, a former Broadway actor and vaudeville performer. Italian in origin, "Rialto" once was a popular name for theaters in the United States.

Sekiu (Strait). The name of a small community, river and point is derived from the original Indian designation, charted by Capt. Henry Kellett and confirmed by George Davidson of the U.S. Coast Survey.

Sequim Bay (Strait). The bay and small city which bears its name come from a Clallam Indian word meaning "quiet waters." In 1841 the Wilkes Expedition christened it Budd's Harbor for Thomas A. Budd, acting master of the *Peacock*. In 1847, Capt. Henry Kellett gave it the name Washington Harbor on British Admiralty charts, and the name was adopted in the 1858 U.S. Coast Survey. But the United States Board of Geographic Names ruled that Washington's name could not be used on minor features that had nothing to do with "The Father of His Country."

Shi Shi Beach (North Coast). This is an anglicized version of its Makah Indian name, *Sh'ah-sha-ees,* meaning "smelt beach" or "surf beach."

Slip Point (Strait). The point's broken formation and frequent slides gives rise to the name. Manuel Quimper named it *Punta de Rojas* in 1791.

Tatoosh Island (Strait). Capt. John Meares named the rocky island after being entertained there by Chief Tatootche. The island is the legendary home of Thunder Bird, and the Chinook name means "Thunder Bird" or "nourishing beast." In Makah, it is called *Tututsh*. In 1790, Manuel Quimper named it *Isla de Tutusi*.

Teahwhit Head (North Coast). The name comes from the Indian name, *T-seal-tla-ok,* meaning "creek falling over a high bluff."

Toke Point (South Coast). Early settlers named the point after an old Indian chief who was an expert canoe navigator and guide.

Toleak Point (North Coast). The name is based on the Clallam Indian word for mussel, *To-luks,* which is what they called the point.

Tongue Point (Strait). This descriptive name was placed on British Admiralty charts in 1847 by Capt. Henry Kellett.

Waada Island (Strait). This is a variation on the Makah Indian name for the island, which has been spelled variously as *Waa-dah, Waaddah, Wa-dah* and *Wa-a-dah*. It was named Neah Island by Cmdr. Charles Wilkes, for the bay in which it is located. In 1846, Capt. Henry Kellett charted it as Wyadda Island.

Waatch Point (North Coast). The point is named for a tribal branch of the Makah Indians; the village of Waatch, pronounced *Wa-a-tch,* no longer exists. Gov. Stevens used the name in a treaty of Jan. 31, 1855.

Westport (South Coast). The name is descriptive of the fishing and crabbing center's location. Previous names included Peterson's Point, Chehalis City and Ft. Chehalis, the latter for a fort established in 1860, before the town was platted. The fort was to protect settlers from Indian attacks, but never was used.

Willapa Bay (South Coast). Named for the Whilapa Indians who lived there when white explorers first arrived, the large, shallow bay has had many monikers. Spanish explorer Jose Martinez de Zayas charted it as *Ensenada de Mal Arrio;* early settlers called it South Bay, as suggested by James Swan. On July 5, 1788, Capt. John Meares gave it the descriptive title, Shoalwater Bay, which later was switched to the present name.

Sources: *Gods & Goblins: A Field Guide to Place Names of Olympic National Park*, by Smitty Parratt (Port Angeles: CP Publications, 1984); *Place Names of Washington*, by Robert Hitchman (Tacoma: Washington Historical Society, 1985).

SOURCES

BOOKS & REPORTS

Alt, David D., and Donald W. Hyndman. *Roadside Geology of Washington*. Missoula: Mountain Press Publishing Co., 1984.

Battelle-Northwest. *Summary Report of a Study on the Future of the Long Beach Peninsula Seashore*. Richland, Wash.: Battelle Memorial Institute, Pacific Northwest Laboratories, 1970.

Brown, Bruce. *Mountain in the Clouds: A Search for the Wild Salmon*. New York: Simon & Schuster, 1982.

Coues, Elliott, ed. *The History of the Lewis and Clark Expedition,* Vol. II. New York: Dover Publications.

Cousteau, Jacques-Yves. *The Cousteau Almanac: An Inventory of Life on Our Water Planet*. Garden City, N.Y.: Doubleday & Co., 1981.

Crowell, Sandra A. *Whaling Off the Washington Coast*. Hoquiam: Washingtonian Print, 1983.

Dana, James D. *Manual of Geology,* 4th ed. New York: American Book Co., 1894.

Darwin, Charles R. *The Voyage of the Beagle*. New York: Bantam Books Inc., 1972.

Douglas, William O. *My Wilderness: The Pacific West*. Garden City: Doubleday & Co., 1960.

Engstrand, Iris H.W. *Spanish Scientists in the New World: the Eighteenth-Century Expeditions*. Seattle and London: University of Washington Press, 1981.

Ernst, Alice Henson. *The Wolf Ritual of the Northwest Coast*. Eugene: The University Press, 1952.

Espy, Willard R. *Oysterville: Roads to Grandpa's Village*. New York: Clarkson N. Potter, Inc., 1977.

Everitt, Robert D., et al. *Marine Mammals of Northern Puget Sound and the Strait of Juan de Fuca: a Report on Investigations November 1, 1977-October 31, 1978*. NOAA Technical Memorandum ERL MESA-41, Boulder, Colo.: 1979.

Feagans, Raymond J. *The Railroad That Ran by the Tide*. San Diego: Howell-North Books, 1981.

Fletcher, Elizabeth Huelsdonk. *The Iron Man of the Hoh: The Man, Not the Myth*. Port Angeles, Wash.: Creative Communications, 1979.

Fluharty, David. *1982-1983 El Niño Task Force Summary*. Seattle: Institute for Marine Studies, University of Washington, 1984.

Franklin, Jerry F., et. al. *Ecological Characteristics of Old-Growth Douglas-Fir Forests*. Pacific Northwest Forest and Range Experiment Station General Technical Report PNW-118. Portland: 1981.

Gibbs, James A. *Pacific Graveyard,* 3rd ed. Portland: Binfords & Mort, 1964.

Gibbs, James A. *Sentinels of the Pacific Northwest*. Portland: Binfords & Mort, 1955.

Gibbs, James A. *Shipwrecks off Juan de Fuca*. Portland: Binfords & Mort, 1968.

Glover, Sheldon L. *Preliminary Report on Petroleum and Natural Gas in Washington*. Washington State Division of Geology Report of Investigations No. 4. Olympia: 1936.

Hart, J.L. *Pacific Fishes of Canada*. Fisheries Research Board of Canada, Bulletin 180. Ottawa: 1973.

Hitchman, Robert. *Place Names of Washington*. Tacoma: Washington State Historical Society, 1985.

Howison, Lieut. Neil M. *Oregon: A Report* (facsimile ed.). Fairfield, Wash.: Ye Galleon Press, 1967.

Hult, Ruby El. *The Untamed Olympics*. Portland: Binfords & Mort, 1971.

Ingmanson, Dale E., and William J. Wallace. *Oceanography: An Introduction,* 2nd ed. Belmont, Calif.: Wadsworth Publishing Co., 1979.

Kozloff, Eugene N. *Seashore Life of the Northern Pacific Coast*. Seattle and London: University of Washington Press, 1983.

Livingston, Vaughn E., Jr. *Oil and Gas Exploration in Washington 1900-1957*. Washington State Division of Mines and Geology Information Circular No. 29. Olympia: 1958.

Lovelock, J. E. *Gaia: A New Look at Life on Earth*. Oxford: Oxford University Press, 1979.

Lupton, Charles T. *Oil and Gas in the Olympic Peninsula, An Extract From U.S.G.S. Bulletin No. 581* (1915). Seattle: Shorey Publications, 1965.

McDonald, Lucile. *Swan Among the Indians*. Portland: Binfords & Mort, 1972.

Maury, Matthew F. *The Physical Geography of the Sea and Its Meteorology*. Cambridge, Mass.: The Belknap Press of Harvard University Press, 1963.

Meany, Edmond S. *Vancouver's Discovery of Puget Sound*. Portland: Binfords & Mort, 1957.

Miller, Russell. *Continents in Collision*. Alexandria, Virginia: Time-Life Books, 1983.

Morgan, Murray. *The Last Wilderness*. Seattle and London: University of Washington Press, 1955.

Newcombe, C. F., ed. *Menzies' Journal of Vancouver's Voyage, April to October, 1792*. Victoria: Archives of British Columbia, 1923.

Newell, Gordon, and Joe Williamson. *Pacific Lumber Ships*. Seattle: Superior Publishing Co., 1960.

Parratt, Smitty. *Gods & Goblins: a Field Guide to Place Names of Olympic National Park*. Port Angeles, Wash.: CP Publications, 1984.

Price, A. Grenfell, ed. *The Explorations of Captain James Cook in the Pacific as Told by Selections of His Own Journals 1768-1779*. New York: Dover Publications, 1971.

Rau, Weldon W. *Geology of the Washington Coast between Point Grenville and the Hoh River*. Washington Department of Natural Resources, Geology and Earth Resources Division, Bulletin No. 66. Olympia, Wash.: 1973.

Rau, Weldon W. *Washington Coastal Geology between the Hoh and Quillayute Rivers*. Washington Department of Natural Resources, Geology and Earth Resources Division, Bulletin No. 72. Olympia, Wash.: 1980.

Reid, George K. *Ecology of Inland Waters and Estuaries*. New York: Reinhold Publishing Corp. 1961.

Rice, Dale W., and Allen A. Wolman. *The Life History and Ecology of the Gray Whale* (Eschrichtius robustus). The American Society of Mammalogists, Special Publication No. 3. Stillwater, Okla.: 1971.

Richmond, Henry R. *The History of the Portland District Corps of Engineers— 1871-1969*. Portland: U.S. Army District, Portland, Corps of Engineers. 1970.

Ricketts, Edward F., and Jack Calvin. *Between Pacific Tides,* 4th ed., revised by Joel W. Hedgpeth. Stanford, Calif.: Stanford University Press, 1968.

Russell, Jervis, ed. *Jimmy Come Lately: History of Clallam County.* Port Angeles, Wash: Clallam County Historical Society, 1971.

Scammon, Charles M. *The Marine Mammals of the Northwestern Coast of North America.* New York: Dover Publications, 1968.

Shawa, Azmi, et. al. *Cranberry Production in the Pacific Northwest.* Pacific Northwest Cooperative Extension Bulletin, PNW-247. Pullman, Wash.: 1984.

Shelton, John S. *Geology Illustrated.* San Francisco: W.H. Freeman, 1966.

Swan, James G. *Almost out of the World: Scenes in Washington Territory.* Tacoma: Washington State Historical Society, 1971.

Swan, James G. *The Indians of Cape Flattery,* facsimile ed. Seattle: Shorey Publications, 1964.

Swan, James G. *The Northwest Coast or, Three Years' Residence in Washington Territory.* Seattle and London: University of Washington Press, 1972.

Tabor, Rowland W. *Guide to the Geology of Olympic National Park.* Seattle and London: University of Washington Press, 1975.

Turekian, Karl K. *Oceans.* Englewood Cliffs, N.J.: Prentice-Hall, Inc., 1968.

Van Syckle, Edwin. *They Tried To Cut It All.* Seattle: Pacific Search Press, 1980.

Van Syckle, Edwin. *The River Pioneers: Early Days on Grays Harbor.* Seattle: Pacific Search Press, 1982.

Wagner, Henry R. *Spanish Explorations in the Strait of Juan de Fuca.* New York: AMS Press, 1971.

Weaver, John E., and Frederic E. Clements. *Plant Ecology.* New York and London: McGraw-Hill Book Co., 1938.

Wertheim, Anne. *The Intertidal Wilderness.* San Francisco: Sierra Club Books, 1984.

Whitebrook, Robert B. *Coastal Exploration of Washington.* Palo Alto: Pacific Books, 1959.

Williams, L.R. *Our Pacific County,* facsimile ed. Seattle: Shorey Publications, 1964.

ARTICLES

Carson, Rob. "Island of Broken Dreams." *Pacific Northwest,* Vol. 17 (Jan./Feb.,1983), pp. 34-42.

Dawson, William L. "A Neglected Coast." *The Pacific Monthly,* Vol. 17, No. 2 (1907), pp. 131-138.

Gwinn, Mary Ann. "Return Flight." *Pacific* (April 14, 1985), pp. 14-21.

Harwood, Michael. "Protection for Protection Arrives in Nick of Time." *Audubon,* Vol. 85 (Jan.,1983), pp. 84-89.

Jameson, Ronald J., et al."History and Status of Translocated Sea Otter Populations in North America." *Wildlife Society Bulletin,* Vol. 10 (1982), pp. 100-107.

Lien, Carsten. "The Olympic Boundary Struggle." *The Mountaineer,* Vol. 52, No. 4 (1959), pp. 18-37.

Nadkarni, Nalini. "Roots That Go Out on a Limb." *Natural History,* Vol. 94 (Feb.,1985), pp. 43-48.

Ocean Spray Cranberries Inc. "Excerpts from *Cranberries* Magazine." *The Sou'-wester,* Vol. 18, No. 3 (1983), pp. 59-60.

Raff, Arthur D., and Ronald G. Mason. "Magnetic Survey off the West Coast of North America, 40° N. Latitude to 52° N. Latitude." *The Geological Society of America Bulletin,* Vol. 72, No. 8 (1961), pp. 1267-1270.

Horse seining crew, Sand Island, 1914. WOODFIELD PHOTO, ILWACO HERITAGE CENTER

Richardson, Elmo R. "Olympic National Park: Twenty Years of Controversy." *Forest History,* Vol. 12, No. 1 (1968), pp. 6-15.

Richardson, Frank. "Breeding Biology of the Rhinoceros Auklet on Protection Island, Washington." *The Condor,* Vol. 63, No. 6 (1961), pp. 456-473.

Scheffer, Victor B. "The Sea Otter on the Washington Coast." *Pacific Northwest Quarterly,* October 1940, pp. 370-388.

Scheffer, Victor B., and John W. Slipp. "The Whales and Dolphins of Washington State with a Key to the Cetaceans of the West Coast of North America." *The American Midland Naturalist,* Vol. 39, No. 2 (1948), pp. 257-337.

Stepankowsky, Andre. "Lost World." *Washington: The Evergreen State Magazine,* Vol 2, No. 3 (1985), pp. 58-62.

Terich, Thomas A., and Maurice L. Schwartz. "A Geomorphic Classification of Washington State's Pacific Coast." *Shore and Beach,* Vol. 49, No. 3 (1981), pp. 21-27.

Terich, Thomas A., and Terrance Levenseller. "The Severe Erosion of Cape Shoalwater, Washington." *Journal of Coastal Research,* Vol. 2, No. 4 (1986), pp. 465-477.

Wadkins, Larry. "Sea Otter." *Washington's Wildlife, Small Game Report,* 1970-1971, pp. 149-154.

Weathers, Larry. "D.J. Crowley and the Cranberry Research Station." *The Sou'-wester,* Vol. 18, No. 3 (1983), pp. 56-59.

Weathers, Larry. "100 Years of Cranberry Farming in Pacific County." *The Sou'-wester,* Vol. 18, No. 3 (1983), pp. 43-52.

Washington Geographic Series

WASHINGTON: THE PEOPLE, THEIR LAND

To know Washington is to see the land—its forms, its weather, its vegetative and wildlife cover. But to really understand Washington is to listen to its people through interviews and to see Washingtonians in their environments. This is a creative and thoughtful look at the whole state—the big view because the landscape is so big. The story is as diverse, insightful, sensitive and occasionally argumentative as Washingtonians' own opinions about their place, its economy, its aspirations, its joys, its exasperations. Colorful, lively, entertaining, reflective—anything but superficial. You'll want this book for border-to-border understanding of Washington's land and people.

JANIS E. BURGER PHOTOS

About the Washington Geographic Series

This series is your guide to enjoying and understanding Washington's places, people and landscapes.

Color photography of the unspoiled country of Washington illustrates every book, and each text is written especially for this series to help you explore, experience and learn about this fascinating state.

WRITE TO:
AMERICAN GEOGRAPHIC PUBLISHING
P.O. BOX 5630
HELENA, MT 59604
(406) 443-2842
Idaho • Montana • Oregon • Washington • Wyoming

Titles in production or planning are:

Washington's Columbia River

Washington's Cascade Range

Washington's San Juan Islands

Order early: Pre-publication discounts are available.

Please send us suggestions for titles you would like to see and your comments about what you see in this volume.